The Memoirs of Nahum N. Glatzer

The Memoirs
of
Nahum N. Glatzer

Edited and Presented by

Michael Fishbane
Judith Glatzer Wechsler

Hebrew Union College Press, *Cincinnati*
in association with
The Leo Baeck Institute, *New York*

Library of Congress Cataloging-in-Publication Data
Glatzer, Nahum Norbert, 1903–1990
The memoirs of Nahum N. Glatzer/edited and
presented by Michael Fishbane and Judith Glatzer Wechsler.
p. cm. – (Jewish perspectives:6)
ISBN 0-87820-506-3
1. Glatzer, Nahum Norbert, 1903–1990.
2. Jewish historians – Biography.
I. Fishbane, Michael A., 1943– II. Wechsler, Judith, 1940–
DS 115.9.G58A3 1997
296'.092 – dc21
[B]   97-25622
           CIP

Design and typography by Noel Martin
Composition by Kelby and Teresa Bowers
Printed on acid-free paper
Manufactured in the United States of America

Distributed by Wayne State University Press
4809 Woodward Avenue, Detroit, Michigan 48201

Contents

Preface

Nahum Glatzer often cited the Talmudic adage that one should not raise one's voice above the text. My father's model was midrashic, deriving from a text a series of stories and interpretations. In this collection of memoirs, the text is his life, and the stories, fragmentary and allusive, a commentary.

Experiences and encounters, often recounted at dinner time, transformed the personal into the metaphorical. People of whom he spoke took on mythic qualities, but not as archetypes, nor for their renown. He spoke of people in a manner than reminds one at times of Borges: knowledgeable, penetrating, ironic, and pithy. My father appreciated the form people and their lives took. Events and encounters were told with unexpected turns and witty aperçus: his gentle wit a counterpoint to the weight of his concerns. He did not write a continuous narrative, both out of modesty and as an artistic choice. My father was moved by simple human gestures, chance encounters, antidotes to inhumanity. Kafka was the writer closest to his heart and I believe was his model. He writes of Kafka's motif—"Man is an exile and cannot return. . . . What drew me to Kafka was his uncanny penetration into the human condition . . . it is always yourself he is talking about." Like Kafka, my father understood memoirs more as impressions, fragments of life, a series of sketches, rather than a finished story.

Nahum Glatzer was a man of deep religious thought and feeling. The depths for him were biblical and ongoing—the problem of evil, the paradox of the Tree of Knowledge, the Book of Job. My father led a life of dialogue with tradition, keeping faith in Judaism in times of radical upheaval. He did not expect divine answers. It is up to us to instill life with acts of faith and lovingkindness. He wrote to me in 1960 while I was studying in Jerusalem:

> *The universe demonstrates law and order and thus the working of an Intelligence but not necessarily a personal principle, a Thou; this is my own thinking in the last decade or so. The universe is utterly neutral. Not so "our" world, our life. Here we have a choice. We may understand it in terms of the neutral impersonal universe (atheism), or we may view it as a realm that admits the personal; it is in this realm where we may discover the divine. (Since there is this choice, we must be entirely honest with ourselves.)*

6

and in another letter:

> *You see, it is Buber's "concrete situation," "responsibility," the obligation*
> *to the Thou that I interpret. I am sure you will find the way to that,*
> *if only after searching and struggle. Without this Thou — the fellow-*
> *man, the divine — we are isolated and lost.*

In the exilic life he led, first by necessity and then by choice, he reflected
on the irony that those not in exile have lost touch with what Judaism is.

> *On your discussion on golah [Diaspora] and Israel: I see again how*
> *difficult, even impossible it is for an Israeli to understand the*
> *position of Diaspora. Reason: lack of knowledge, or rather, direct*
> *experience. The issue cannot be decided from a mere Israeli*
> *theory of what Judaism is.*

He suggests the paradox: those not in exile are in spiritual exile.

My father kept diaries all his life, not intended for the eyes of others. Ini-
tially, and occasionally afterward, they were encoded, German written in
Greek letters. The diaries were a way of dealing with isolation. But in his
later years, he began to write what he called his memoirs, mainly during
sabbatical terms or summer "vacations" taken at my mother's urging. The
entries were written during 1971, 1972, 1978, and 1980, on individual 5 x 7
inch sheets kept in a box marked *zichronot*/memoirs. Each piece is dated,
but no order was set. Some sections were revised by him years later, providing some translations and explanations.

In the present selection the 78 entries have been divided into three
parts, of which the first two are roughly chronological. In the first part,
the memories of his early years elucidate my father's religious path from
strict Orthodoxy with its Talmudic study in Eastern Europe to a more historical, cultural, and aesthetic understanding of Judaism encountered in
Frankfurt, first as a student and then as a teacher. He was concerned with
reconciling secular life with the sacred. There are entries up until events
in 1980 and a reflection on the course of his scholarly career in the section "Midrash." The second part, called "Encounters," contains anecdotal
and at times humorous accounts of some of the key figures in twentieth-
century Jewry whom my father knew, among them S. Y. Agnon, Martin
Buber, Franz Rosenzweig, and Salman Schocken. Particular pleasure is

taken in moments in which they are caught off guard. The final section is concerned with the faces of faith.

These memoirs are a testimony to a life lived in the arena of history by one who moved from language to language, country to country, sphere to sphere, in the conjunction of the personal and the public. They reveal a wisdom born of scholarship, tempered by life, and leavened by irony and gentle wit. Anecdotal, aphoristic, poignant, they give a sense of Nahum Glatzer's appreciation of the paradoxical and the improbable.

My father indicated that these memoirs were a document for the family. The idea for their publication came from Rabbi Ben Zion Gold, who stressed their historical significance. I hope my father would not have objected. I think they were written to be read. Professor Michael Fishbane worked with my mother and me in the preparation of the manuscript, providing not only the explanatory notes but also the introduction, giving an historical and scholarly context from the perspective of a former student and colleague. I am grateful for his dedication to this project.

The memoirs reveal a different dimension of my father, complementary to his scholarship, recounting worlds since passed whose legacy we strive to remember and whose spirit revive.

— Judith Glatzer Wechsler

Introduction

A teaching in the Jerusalem Talmud says that when a student transmits something in the name of his teacher, he should imagine his teacher's face and behold it while reporting the tradition. This is a sacred duty – a duty of piety to one's teacher and a demand of faithfulness to the past. But it is also a reminder that learning comes from teachers who, through their presence and voice, embody the past in a living way. Nahum Glatzer was such an honest servant of tradition and memory, and his face is before me now as I attempt to convey something of his remarkable life of learning and teaching. I have no doubt that his image is also etched on the hearts of all those who knew and loved him, and who learned from him how the texts of Jewish religious history could become a source of inner power and personal destiny for the patient, attentive student.

In a revealing personal aside, Franz Kafka once remarked, "I am a memory come alive."[1] The same could be said of the memoirist, who ponders the landscape of a life. Shaped by the experiences one has lived through and formulated as fragments of identity, the memoir is something like a second living. The fundamental past is revived – but in an older heart and mind whose ongoing life bears witness to its formative significance. There is thus something particularly poignant in the memoirist's summing up of a lifetime – a "coming alive" to oneself for a final time, and a recreation from disparate events of a sustained "I am."

But rarely and preciously, one's memories may be paradigmatic as well for a certain course of history. Then the personal memoir may invoke a collective "I am." Just this, I believe, is the case with the memoirs of Nahum Glatzer collected here. Reflecting the rich and vigorous life of one who experienced the complex movement of Jewish existence from tradition to modernity and enjoyed the friendship of some of the most remarkable Jews of the age, these recollections are a unique document by any standard. They are the product of Glatzer's final decades – from sundry times and circumstances. As typical of the man, the facts were all duly recorded in their season in detailed diaries and daybooks; but the motivation to give his notes a voice came in response to the family's request for a more permanent record of his life. Nevertheless, features of the manuscript and its style suggest that Glatzer knew his place in history and the particular historical value of his private reminiscences. Just how much this sensibility guided his hand and expression we shall never know. What we do know is that otherwise irretrievable vignettes, voices, and events of the past come alive in these pages in unanticipated ways, and this is a great and precious gift. Those who knew him will quickly recognize the characteristic candor and cadence of his voice — but especially the honest eye of one who saw much. The deeply private Glatzer was a man filled with memories. They are presented here in carefully crafted words.

⁓

Nahum Norbert Glatzer was born on March 25, 1903 in Lemberg (Lvov), Galicia and grew up in a deeply pious and traditional atmosphere. His father was his first and most influential model of a life guided by faith and humility.[2] But other figures also had a dramatic impact upon him. Glatzer recalled two teachers of this sort — one, sometime near the outbreak of the First World War, lived in a room bare of all earthly essentials but a chair, a table and a Talmud; the other lived in the most abject poverty and once startled the young boy with the question why did God give him two hands, and with the equally unexpected answer that one was to mark the text, while the other was to point to the commentaries for guidance.[3] Glatzer absorbed these images of modest dignity and made them part of his own inner truth.

In the unsettled atmosphere that sundered communities at the outbreak of the Great War, the young Glatzer began the first of many exilic wanderings. After an initial period in Tetchen (Bohemia), his father ultimately determined upon the city of Bodenbach in the hopes of retaining a traditional atmosphere, although very few of the Jews there (beside the refugees) were observant. This parental decision meant that Glatzer could continue his secular studies at the local Gymnasium, alongside his Talmudic tutorials. This combination had a decisive impact upon him. He soon developed the notion that it was up to him to preserve Judaism among this remnant and to teach it in ways responsive to the hour and its needs. And this he did amidst a group of fellow students known as the *Matteh Aaron* (Aaron's Staff), to whom he taught the classics of Judaism along with translations and specimens of wisdom from the broader world of Jewish and secular learning.[4]

The materials young Glatzer developed for the group show a remarkable and distinctive creativity.[5] He produced a small library of pamphlets copied out in an exquisite Hebrew and German hand. Each announced its subject on the title page, with its author or editor. The materials included sermons for the Holy Days, with quotes from the classical sources, historical information, and bits of moral guidence; anthologies of translations from medieval Hebrew poetry (ibn Ezra being a favorite) and excerpts from historical books (like Heinrich Graetz's classic work) and from various books of the Bible (like Lamentations) as well as Rashi's commentary (to Leviticus). In addition, Glatzer composed original Bible commentaries, including exegetical and philological remarks on the book of Judges and annotations to the sacrificial rites found in the book of Leviticus. And beyond all this there are also excerpts from his broad reading in the history of religions (e.g., a forgotten study on the Baal Shem Tov and Jewish monism) and discussions of selected topics (e.g., the Babylonian myth of creation, with numerous terms in the original). It is hard to conceive all this as the educational project of a young person – eager to provide his students with booklets that were both scholarly and aesthetic. But so they are. Remarkably, Glatzer the lover and editor of books is already evident here, as is his vision of a Judaism that draws from the well of tradition and remains open to all knowledge. A synthesis of the religious and literary imagination has seemingly burst nearly fully formed from his head. Perhaps the influential essay by S. H. Bergman (entitled "Kiddusch Ha-Schem") provided some literary inspiration, as he suggests; but living examples of this new blend of Jewish spirituality were not so easily found, and certainly not in Bodenbach.[6]

For this one would have to go elsewhere, like Heppenheim, located just outside Frankfurt. There lived Martin Buber, already famous and influential; and there went the young Glatzer, soon after the war, with his father's permission (and admonition to beware the influence of this freethinker). The circumstances that led to Glatzer's request for an interview may be reconstructed from the letter he sent in 1920 to Buber (addressed as *geehrter Meister* [revered master]) in advance of his visit, and from the memoirs and personal reports.[7] According to the letter, Glatzer wished to discuss his concerns for a revitalized Judaism and mentions his readings in classical texts and modern Jewish writers. But from the later writings we learn that he also intended to discuss his own thoughts regarding Buber's translations of Hasidic teachings. One can only marvel at Glatzer's youthful temerity. In the event, however, the meeting was a short one — despite the intense period of preparation that preceded it. Overwhelmed by the personal presence and "deep eyes"of the "great Jew," Glatzer blurted out that Buber's stylistic renditions misrepresented the rough quality of the original sources. In Glatzer's recollection, Buber became somewhat defensive about his translations, and the hoped-for encounter turned into a mismeeting.[8]

An enduring connection was nevertheless established soon thereafter, and continued for some fifty years — as Glatzer served Buber (and Rosenzweig) as special assistant in their Bible translation, studied intensively with Buber as a seminar student and doctoral candidate (eventually succeeding his mentor in the position in Jewish Religious Thought and Social Ethics at the University of Frankfurt), and was a major catalyst in the dissemination of Buber's works in America in the 1960s. In all these roles Glatzer remained respectful and devoted, but never failed to give Buber sharp and honest reactions when he felt it necessary. Particularly poignant was Glatzer's rebuke (after Rosenzweig's death) that Buber had improperly downplayed Rosenzweig's collaboration in the translation project by the way he referred to their work on the title page.[9] The first meeting was thus prophetic. Equally significant was the meeting of eyes. Several photographs from the 1950s show the already mature Glatzer leaning toward Buber in conversation, in deep and attentive gaze.

Many years later Glatzer would say that his contact with great men gave him perspective — and humility. One such influential figure was Rabbi Nehemiah A. Nobel. Although the young Glatzer first went to the Breuer Yeshivah in Frankfurt to fulfill his father's desire that he become an Orthodox rabbi, the style and atmosphere of the learning there were not to his liking (an official holiday photo of the boys in his group shows him half-hidden near the rear), and he soon found himself attending the morning services and Talmud study session in Nobel's home. Here was a new atmosphere rich in literary and cultural references (especially Goethe), which the learned and worldly Nobel would infuse into the discussions of rabbinic literature. Similarly, Nobel's Sabbath sermons were equally filled with Jewish and literary passions, often rising to near-prophetic thunder ("the Spirit as 'cloudburst'").[10] In all this, the young Glatzer found embodied the combination of tradition and universal knowledge he had intuited on his own.[11] The moral energies and historical learning of fellow students such as Ernst Simon, Siegfried Kracauer and Leo Lowenthal also made an impression and confirmed that here was the new Judaism of his longing.[12] Soon Glatzer said a decisive No to the Breuer Yeshivah and took on his Hebrew name of Nahum at Nobel's suggestion. This Yes was in every way a new direction and new birth.

Another student in Rabbi Nobel's Talmud group had an even more decisive impact. That was Franz Rosenzweig, who had only recently come to Frankfurt after the war (in 1919), and who was urged by Nobel himself to stay in that city and be involved in the *Volkshochschule* (Institute of Adult Jewish Education), whose establishment was then in the planning stage.[13] Glatzer was deeply affected by the force of Rosenzweig's personality and became his devoted friend and life-long disciple. Innumerable activities bound their lives together. Glatzer regarded Rosenzweig's powers of thinking and learning with awe, and many times in later years Glatzer would refer to Rosenzweig as a "genius." Indeed Glatzer often expressed deep amazement at Rosenzweig's ability to absorb as much Jewish study as he had in the short period between his "return" to Judaism and the composition of his *Star of Redemption* several years later. This massive learning is evidenced in the list of Jewish sources that Glatzer compiled (at Rosenzweig's suggestion) for the second edition. The supplement also gives a hint of the erudition Glatzer himself possessed — for at best the classical Jewish references in the *Star* are merely alluded to, and never cited. Glatzer's control of texts from all periods and genres made him an invaluable aide to the Buber-Rosenzweig Bible translation; tracking down sources and finding overlooked comments was one of his tasks.[14] And somewhat later, when Buber and S.Y. Agnon (a Nobel laureate in Literature) needed an assistant in their projected compilation of a corpus of Hasidic materials, once again "young Glatzer" was the obvious choice.[15]

But it was not simply (or ultimately) the book learning of Rosenzweig that attracted Glatzer. Far more compelling was his sagacity and humor. All these served as models of a new Judaism. When Rosenzweig established the new Center for Jewish study in Frankfurt (the *Freies Jüdisches Lehrhaus*) to propagate an open and nonapologetic encounter with the sources of Jewish thought and faith, Glatzer was one of its first instructors in Bible and Midrash — and its most careful chronicler over many years.[16] Interaction with such fellow teachers as Buber himself, Ernst Simon, Erich Fromm, Rudolf Hallo, Ludwig Strauss, and even Gershom Scholem produced an electrifying atmosphere. All questions were opened, all theological matters discussed, and all care was exacted to hear texts and students (in the right but varying proportions) speaking in their own voice. Texts were teachers and teachers texts; students were teachers and the teachers students. The classroom became the center of living Torah — as revelation was heard in written and oral forms. For a select few there were even more intense and unforgettable experiences. One was a small seminar conducted by Gershom Scholem on the Zohar, and commentaries on the messianic sections of the book of Daniel (the meetings began at midnight); another was (in 1922) when some of the Hebraists heard Agnon read from his story *Aggadat Ha-Sofer* (The Legend of the Scribe). The "voice and tenor" of that "reading" entered Glatzer's ear forever: "it was reverent, humble, submissive, but not tragic."[17] Several years earlier (in 1917), a comparably young Gershom Scholem heard Agnon read the same story before the *Bet Ha-Va'ad Ha-Ivri Klub* in Berlin, and his "delicate, plaintive voice" made a similarly "profound impression."[18] These moments of learning and listening were received by Glatzer as a precious gift, which he transmitted through his own voice and being to generations of students.

Indeed, the challenge of the "New Learning" and "New Thinking" embodied in the Lehrhaus was to put knowledge and intellect to the service of patient listening to the voice of texts — and to the service of life, in whatever shape that might take. Such "service" was in fact the revolutionary principle in Rosenzweig's well-known letter to his mentor, the historian Friedrich Meinecke, when he firmly declined the offer of an academic position and career;[19] and such service was the core of Rosenzweig's life in the Lehrhaus and his radiation of the truth of his Jewish learning through nobility and humor during the long period of his fatal illness.[20] The concept was internalized by Glatzer as a life-long ideal of teaching, discipline, and devotion.[21] As he noted near the end of his life, service as the spiritual embodiment of the truths of Judaism was modelled first and foremost by his father, but also heroically and humbly by Rosenzweig. The spirits of both men lived in Glatzer's soul and were revived in heart and mind through his lifetime.

Glatzer recalled poignantly how Rosenzweig had cried when he told him that his father was killed during an Arab riot on Moza (a village outside Jerusalem) in 1929; and during the years of Rosenzweig's illness, Glatzer served his friend with loving devotion and acted as cantor in the intimate circle of prayer that formed around the master's bed.[22] There was a haunting martyrological aura to Rosenzweig's final suffering and death; and Glatzer wrote of it in a magisterial Hebrew essay. Glatzer often showed images of that time to his students. When they came to his home, he invited them upstairs to his study. Across the room was a photograph of Rosenzweig harnessed to his chair, from which he indicated with eye movements his intentions and concerns. The heroic magnitude of his commitment to life was compelling beyond words. From a lower panel in a bookcase Glatzer would produce the death mask. Its presence always seemed a revelation of human transcendence; and it was at this moment that we sensed how one face, one life, could transfigure another.

Frankfurt was the "beloved" home for Glatzer — the place to which he returned eagerly after brief holy day periods in the silent and unhappy homelife at Elberfeld, or other times nurtured by the hospitality and care of Mrs. Adele Rosenzweig (Franz's mother) in Kassel. He treasured Frankfurt for the vitality and intensity of his friendships there, for its library and books and writing projects (translations and feuilletons), and for the rigor and discipline of its University. In the course of preparations for his university qualifying exams, Glatzer quipped that he had fallen in love with "Orientalia," a maiden whose enchantments held him in thrall. Hebraica of all sorts was a personal passion; but devotion to Arabic language and literature (under the stern tutelage of Professor Josef Horovitz)[23] made one of the deepest impressions upon him, and he also felt the allure of Aramaic and Assyriology. A serious student of philology, Glatzer never forgot the precision that careful language study inculcates; but he also kept in mind the lessons of the Lehrhaus and the importance of hearing the particular voice of the text and its address.

Under the direction of Martin Buber, Glatzer wrote his dissertation on the Tannaitic conception of history (*Untersuchungen zur Geschichtslehre der Tannaiten: Ein Beitrag zur Religionsgeschichte*, 1932).[24] This still unparalleled study examines its subject with phenomenological and typological precision and reveals the historical imagination of the ancient sages in its many forms and concerns. Significantly, it is always the voice of a rabbi, an embodied individual at a particular moment, who speaks through the words of Scripture and tries to actualize them for historical times (past, present, and future). Buber's influence is keenly felt in the negative contrast drawn between these expressions and the apocalyptic imagination (of Fourth Ezra), in which time is not open to existential challenges but fated and predetermined.[25] Glatzer further drew from Buber the perception that, for the Tannaim, history was preeminently a dialogue between God and man, one that would receive its final confirmation only in redemption. But even for this dialogical dimension Glatzer owed much to Rosenzweig, whose thoughts on the relationship between history and redemption appear at the conclusion of the work. Nahum Glatzer succeeded Buber at Frankfurt University; but he dedicated his dissertation to the memory of Franz Rosenzweig.

For Glatzer and his great teachers, the tumult of time was to be resisted through faithful commitment to spiritual goals. Several early translations of rabbinic legends gave witness to this truth of Jewish history;[26] but Glatzer's mastery of the sources and his ability to arrange them anthologically with artistic and pedagogical force were decisively manifested in his first and valuable anthology *Ein jüdisches Lesebuch. Sendung und Schicksal. Aus dem Schrifttum des nachbiblischen Judentums* (with Ludwig Strauss).[27] A collection on the destiny and fate of Israel, it was intended to complement another on modern Judaism compiled by Strauss, and was undertaken, mostly by Glatzer, after the Strauss anthology was completed. The sources are arranged thematically (not historically), and focus on the inner life of piety, decision, and uprightness that shape both the acts of the individual Jew and the ideals of the people. The materials range from anonymous folk renditions to the self-conscious formulations of philosophers — with much in between. Everything collected here has lasted in the mind of the people and shaped its destiny; every word has the pulse of a voice and the revelation of tradition; and the variety of materials show a Judaism with eyes and hands in heaven and on earth: in time and eternity. In Glatzer's presentation, beginnings are not in the creation of the world, but in the decision of the heart to change and act on the ideals of piety. Teachers do not demand, but instruct by example and proverb. And faith is not only steadfastness in degrading times, but also polemical assurance, inner resistance to tyranny, and the sanctification of God on earth. For Glatzer, these are the ideals towards which a Jew strives before the end of earthly days.

The diversity of sources in this collection indicates the range of possibilities for the modern Jew, who may hear a trace of the voice meant for him alone. This presentation of the richness of Jewish religious expression

was a vital and enduring tenet for Glatzer, and one that he held to steadfastly all his life. It reveals his utterly undogmatic vision of Judaism, as
well as his confidence that its sources may break through the noise of the
everyday and give one a spiritual direction and higher calling. Indeed, the
potential of the sources to give spiritual and cultural strength was a fervent hope of Glatzer the teacher. In this regard it is notable that an English
version of *Sendung und Schicksal* appeared in America immediately after
the Second World War (1946) and, together with some organizational re-
arrangements and the addition of Hasidic materials, contains more material on Jewish martyrology.[28] Nothing is said directly about the events
underlying this inclusion; that would be to overteach the sources and pre-
determine the reader's response. Such was not Glatzer's way. More cir-
cumspectly, he speaks of a conception of human life revealed in the documents "as one great dialogue between man and God"; and about a sense
of "the deep concern and reverence with which the authors approached
matters of life and spirit."[29]

Nevertheless, Nahum Glatzer clearly knew that the evils of the time just
passed required examples of a community dedicated to sanctity and value
– for the sake of contrast and instruction. Thus in a later edition of the
original German anthology (in 1969, with slight revisions),[30] Glatzer gave
this expression to his lifelong vision: "Are these testimonies to Jewish tradition of value in a world in which values have become more than questionable? No one can say that easy answers to the questions of our era are
to be found here. And yet these texts are more than mere historical records. They may contribute toward keeping alive the memory of a community which has attempted – in spite of history – to lead a life of faith."

Glatzer was a master editor, who knew that virtually all the great
sources of Judaism are anthologies, gathered fragments from the tablets
of the past and hewed into a new whole. They were "a memory come alive"
on the page and in the heart, and gave strength to Glatzer himself in his
next series of moves. With decisive prescience he and Anne, recently married, left Germany in 1933 and went to London. Glatzer thus forfeited the
only university position of Judaica in Germany just before news of his formal dismissal was published in the press. While in England, Professor Herbert Loewe was able to secure for him a position at the University of London; but Glatzer declined, preferring to go to Palestine and build his academic future there. He accepted a post at the Reali Gymnasium in Haifa,

famous for its rigorous high school training and esteemed faculty.[31] Under difficult conditions Glatzer continued to produce a variety of scholarly works, including his original and instructive presentation of Maimonides' thought (*Rabbi Mosche ben Maimon: Eine systematischer Querschnitt durch sein Werk*, 1935);[32] a brief but remarkable anthology of midrashic sayings that capture the directness, profundity, and paradoxes of the ancient rabbinic mind (*Gespräche der Weisen: Aus Talmudischen-Midraschischen Texten*, 1935);[33] his lucid historical account of ancient Talmudic times (*Geschichte der talmudischen Zeit*, 1937);[34] dozens of rabbinic sayings ("Merksprüche") formulated for the German reading public (in the *Jüdische Rundschau*, 1935–37);[35] and a host of translations from the contemporary works of S.Y. Agnon (these appeared from 1933 through 1938). In all these ways, Glatzer contributed to the spiritual resistance of German Jews in darkest times.[36]

In the course of the next years, Glatzer gradually and reluctantly realized that a university position in the Land of Israel was neither an imminent nor a realistic option, and with the earlier offer of a position in London no longer viable, he went to the United States — though at that time there were practically no positions in Jewish Studies outside of seminaries. In the 1940s Glatzer lived in Chicago, Boston, and New York, and taught rabbinic literature at the Hebrew Theological College in Chicago and the Hebrew Teachers College in Boston, as well as ancient Greek and Roman history at Yeshiva University in New York. During this period he was invited by the publisher Salman Schocken to become editor-in-chief of the newly reorganized Schocken Books in New York, and thus an older association with the former Berlin publisher was revived and expanded. Schocken's vision of a book (its feel and form), his understanding of its potential cultural power, and his exacting work ethic greatly appealed to Glatzer.[37] He nevertheless firmly resisted Schocken's attempts to seduce him away from academia entirely and devote himself to the more "realistic" world of publishing. But through his decades-long position as editor, Glatzer was able to create a virtual revolution in the production and dissemination of Jewish books of intellectual quality. He continued in this important capacity long after he received the offer of a professorate at the newly founded Brandeis University in Waltham, Massachusetts.

Among the first of many projects planned for the spiritual invigoration of American Jewry was the translation and revision of earlier German anthologies. The English rendition of *Sendung und Schicksal* appeared in 1946 under the title *In Time and Eternity: A Jewish Reader*.[38] Soon thereafter came the Midrash reader tellingly called *Hammer on the Rock* (1948), a latter-day incarnation of his earlier *Gespräche*. Nothing like this collection in conception or form had ever been published in America. Through it the breath of the sages called out, dialogically, to the hearer-reader, like some revivification of the original "living messengers" of Talmudic Judaism — teachers "who took the place of inanimate books and could thus preserve all the immediacy of their message without it being exposed to that danger of date and dogma which imperils any book."[39] Here was more than old memories; here was voice, the texture of Scripture, and the dramatic "making of thought and life one all-embracing commentary on the living word of God."[40]

Glatzer's *Hammer* is a magnificent achievement. While perhaps only the expert will fully appreciate the astonishing eye that has culled from a voluminous corpus these facets of faith, every reader will immediately feel their prismatic power. The sayings are arranged in thematic groups, without a hint of editorial artifice. And yet the artful work of a master is there throughout, as in all the great midrashic collections of old. A first pass through the ten sections will reveal its sequential structure: it begins with the creation and the primeval period and moves through the patriarchal cycles and the exodus to the revelation at Sinai and the generations of covenantal life, exile, suffering and redemption. This is the course of biblical time, the theological structure of Judaism. But on closer inspection one will also see that the editor has not taken the obvious teachings about creation or revelation or redemption from rabbinic literature, or simply followed the biblical canonical order. Much more do the teachings convey a spiritual sensibility and reinterpretation of older categories. Creation is knowing the right time, in due season, and returning to such times for the renewal of life; revelation is the hearing of a voice and the seeing of a face, and knowing what to do with time, so that it is not a mass of deadness; and redemption is just that newness of soul that is the gift of love and learning, and the courage to endure evil with patience and a sense of value.

Upon even closer study, the attentive reader becomes aware of the paradoxes of human existence conveyed by the teachings, and by the mixtures of hope and resignation, or will and fatefulness expressed therein. The materials also illuminate the complex purposes of self in community, and, on another level, the despair of suffering and Israel's higher glory. No one view stands alone: they are all in silent dialogue in the same section, and across sections, and sometimes in specific paragraphs. Bialik and Ravnitzky produced their magisterial collection of rabbinic legend, called *Sefer ha-Aggadah*, in the 1920s and 30s, as part of the romantic project of "ingathering" the sources – and did so in grand form and mostly from the midrashic texts found in the Babylonian Talmud.[41] Glatzer's work breathes the same spirit of renewal, but is more richly textured in paradoxes. Here is knowledge as service, performed with modesty and profound wisdom. Many other collections on faith and knowledge in Jewish sources extended Glatzer's role as a teacher for a new American generation. With the subtle silence of an editor, he shaped new sensibilities through his sense of the spiritual power of Judaism.[42] All that was required of the reader was "readiness."

The notion of readiness was of fundamental importance to Rosenzweig, the transformation of whose life through contact with the sources of Judaism was a model for all who knew him. Glatzer knew that the story of Rosenzweig's path to living faith was a compelling one, even beyond its original time and place, and his first major act of intellectual service in America was to bring alive the life and thought of his beloved mentor and companion for the English speaking world. The biography *Franz Rosenzweig. His Life and Thought* (1953) was presented by Nahum Glatzer in the same way he presented the life and thought of the sages: in Rosenzweig's own words, and in accounts of his words; in reports of his deeds, and in testimonies thereof. The editor is unobtrusive; what alone matters is the presentation of a life radiant in courage and sanctity and the dialogue of the sage with friends and God. The account of how the young Rosenzweig decided to remain Jewish after spending Yom Kippur (1913) in an Orthodox synagogue in Berlin was told to Glatzer by Rosenzweig's mother, and has since been glorified into one of the most celebrated reversions to Judaism of modern times.[43] And the accounts of Rosenzweig's creativity and suffering have come, for many, to represent glimpses of the life of a modern saint. Here then was a model for the contemporary seeker: a fully thoughtful and pious person; a theologizing philosopher who valued action over abstraction; a person who grew in observance but condemned all pettiness and dogmatism; and one who exemplified a return to the sources and the simplicity of faith without sacrificing his all-too-human and sophisticated reflection.

Glatzer's biography of Rosenzweig had an important cultural impact from its first appearance – a fact publicly acknowledged in the introduction to the 1966 symposium on "The State of Jewish Belief" in *Commentary* magazine.[44] Glatzer's presentation of Rosenzweig's life and thought has also influenced the subsequent generation of American Jewish theologians. After its initial appearance, Buber chided Glatzer for not doing such a biography of him, and was rebuked with the words that he, Buber, could speak well enough for himself, but that Rosenzweig could not, and that the telling of his life was both a necessity and a piety. And it was.

Such simple directness was characteristic of Glatzer, for all his deeply shy manner. It gave his speech a quality of deliberateness that seemed wrought from profound inner silences. Indeed, for students and colleagues this personal manner seemed to model the sanctity of language – as if Glatzer had undertaken some ascetic vow never to add to the thoughtless noise of the world. The fact that he experienced the meaning of dialogue directly from Buber and Rosenzweig added to the aura he bore. During the nearly twenty years that he taught at Brandeis University, his presence in the classroom was always marked by the measured tone and content of his lectures and by the respectful way he mediated the sources of Jewish life and thought to his students. His lectures were carefully prepared and carried in little notebooks, along with lists of students whose names he was concerned to know and whose characteristics he sometimes noted cryptically (often with Greek letters).

The realities of texts and persons were not abstractions to Glatzer. He acted through his belief. Thus while his whole being often conveyed the impression of a deep and withdrawn absorption, he was directly present to each situation and dealt with it according to its demands. Two personal encounters are indicative. The first occurred just after I served as the assistant for his large lecture course called "Job and the Problem of Evil." At the end of the semester Glatzer expressed gratitude and asked what he could do for me. From some mysterious depth of desire (and certainly expressing the secret wish of my fellow students), I somehow said that I would very much like him to teach me a chapter of Bible in the way he had learned it from Martin Buber. The request was granted, a time was set –

and we soon sat face to face in his office. Glatzer then handed me the text of Exodus, indicated that I should open to the portion of *Va-Yakhel* (the last chapters), and proceeded to fire a succession of questions at me, like, What words strike you? and To what documentary source do modern critics assign them? and Do they have Akkadian cognates? and What more do you hear? Well there I was, armed with the shield of philology, proudly defending the discipline and even adding a thrust or two, but altogether puzzled by what was to be heard. I thought that philological seeing was enough, and didn't at first grasp that Glatzer knew and anticipated my answers but was pushing me to hear the inner vibration of the words and the more complex unities of Scripture. And so without ever dismissing the first (historical) method, I was led to note the verbal texture linking that part of Exodus with the opening chapters of Genesis, and then to explore the theological tenor of this link as teaching something about beginnings, the sanctity of space, and the relationship between human and divine work. Glatzer then cited passages to the same effect from rabbinic literature (the *Tanḥuma* and Midrash *Tadshe*), and showed me the texts themselves. The event was exhausting and unsettling. I asked if this was not only the thread of Buber's teaching but also his tempo. Glatzer said Yes; but I also knew that he had just revealed much of his own rhythm of study as well.

Another instance was conveyed as an unforgettable lesson in scholarly probity and thoroughness. It followed my youthful question of how I could know just what I wanted to work on and how much I should read before I approached one of the faculty as a mentor. Glatzer stared at me. I waited. And then the measured voice:"Well . . . of course you will go to the library, and you will find the books in the BM section, and you will read them, starting where you want, and then you will want to go to the BS section and the PJ has a lot, too. And then I think you will have some idea of what you want, and it will be easy for you to come to one of us with your thoughts." The thunder at Sinai could not have been more frightening than the silence that followed this instruction. Years later, when I asked Glatzer how he viewed the recent proliferation of Jewish Studies positions in America, and what was to him his greatest concern for the future, he turned to me and offered silence. And then he simply said:"Pseudo-scholarship."

Here was authenticity of task, awareness of profound and irresolvable tensions, and the solitude and silence that go with both. After Rosenzweig, Franz Kafka was Nahum Glatzer's most enduring modern model, and he devoted over fifty years to reading and publishing the writer's work (stories and parables, letters and diaries) "out of gratitude."[45] For in Kafka's writing Glatzer found an austere, paradoxical, and parabolic presentation of the modern condition, filled with the demands of authentic writing born of patience and loneliness, and ever in tension with guilt feelings for one's father and faithfulness to one's inner destiny. Kafka knew what it was like to imagine paradise and be without it, to have traditions and transform them, to be a metamorphosed alien in society — and so did Glatzer. The affinity of souls was profound, and even bore on such personal matters as the relationship between knowledge and death, and between the life of action and inaction (contemplation). Moreover, Glatzer believed Kafka to be above all else a Jewish writer and thinker, and some of his most profound works to be "biblical" in theme and concern. He was not alone in this judgment: Rosenzweig once remarked that Kafka's novel *The Castle* reminded him of nothing as much as the Bible;[46] and Gershom Scholem had the same sense, writing to Walter Benjamin that the place to begin any inquiry into Kafka was the Book of Job.[47]

Glatzer was particularly drawn to the thematic of knowledge. In an essay entitled "Franz Kafka and the Tree of Knowledge" (1958), he explored this matter as the kernal of Kafka's thought,[48] finding in his works a deep tension between the life of knowledge and its complications, on the one hand, and the practice of contemplative waiting and patience on the other.[49] In Glatzer's understanding, Kafka had penetrated to the core of the paradoxical relationship between knowledge and the consciousness of death. But he certainly knew that this theme had deeper roots. This is particularly marked in the preface he wrote for his collection *The Dimensions of Job*. In that piece he dealt directly with the Garden of Eden narrative, and discussed the curse of knowledge as the awareness of mortality, as well as the profound recognition Job attains when he grows in wisdom and perceives a measure of theological truth in the vast silences of existence.[50]

Glatzer was justly proud of these two essays (on Kafka and Job), which mirror the web of wisdom he too pondered. Sometime in the mid-1980s, shortly after he retired a second time (in 1985, after a decade of teaching at Boston University), he gave a talk on Kafka's loves, as was his pleasure. At some point he came around to the meaning of Kafka and tersely reported two of Kafka's parables — actually one involuted doublet. In it the writer portrays a runner, himself, bolting down the palace steps and out through the many courts, with a message from the king. He willfully overcomes all obstacles, and hurtles though space with heroic determination for he triumphantly bears some word, some truth, from the recesses. And then the parable ends with a vision of the contemplative self — you, who sit alone by the window, dreaming it all.[51] Glatzer concluded with silence. Those who knew him, and his thoughts about the relations between the *vita activa* and *vita contemplativa* might imagine that his choice of just this paradox was most revealing.

The world of Glatzer's memoirs comes alive in Kafkaesque sequences — in parabolic episodes, haunting and somewhat surreal dreams, paradoxical ironies, and most of all in spare and translucent prose. Each moment is rescued from a silence and shyness that spirals down, we now learn, into echoless eras of childhood.

The present collection is presented in three parts. Part One, entitled "Memories," presents episodes and vignettes from Glatzer's life in chronological sequence. The earliest go back to recollections of his forebears and the conditions of his birth; the latest record moments of acknowledgment by the academic community and personal reflections on his scholarly career. In between are the decades of youth in Eastern and Central Europe; advanced studies and academic development in Western Europe; and subsequent uprootings that led first (briefly) to England, and then to Palestine and the United States. Glatzer's eight decades thus follow an historical curve of wanderings and disruptions due to the two World Wars, and a path from the piety of an older world of tradition to the challenges of modern thought and society. Glatzer moved through these diverse worlds with inner balance and self-direction. Indeed, one frequently notes the incongruity of disjunctive scenes recounted by a narrator filled with purpose and resolve, even as he lived in chaotic times.

Most striking about these memoirs is the complex unity Glatzer constantly achieved between tradition and modernity. Whether it was integrating the sacred studies of Eastern European *melamdim* (Torah scholars) with secular subjects in the Gymnasium, the advanced Talmud study group with modern Semitic philology, or critical Near Eastern Studies with the attentive religiosity characteristic of Rosenzweig's Lehrhaus, the highest and most enduring values of each sphere were retained and integrated. The remarkable prescience of the young man in Bodenbach who formed his Matteh Aaron society to teach and translate selections from the classical tradition and modern cultural thought for his contemporaries presages the renowned teacher and editor of later years who presented diverse teachings of Judaism as witness to a truth of existence that might yet challenge and address the modern individual.

Glatzer held steady to his nondogmatic approach, and had little appreciation for pomposity, glib assurance, and impersonal religious institutions. Except for extraordinary years in the intense atmosphere of the Lehrhaus and the smaller circle that formed around Rosenzweig, Glatzer's spiritual solitude and vocation found social resonance only rarely. Moments of religious community in the synagogue were, for him, but anticipations of fuller messianic harmonies, precious but always partial. His center of gravity was much more an inwardness cultivated by the spiritual tradition of Judaism that he studied. It was from this center that he edited his books and taught his classes.

Part Two, "Encounters," presents another dimension of Glatzer the observer and participant. Here the memoirs are profiles of the many great individuals he knew and interacted with, from his first days in Frankfurt to the final years in Boston. These are all personal presences who were seen and spoken with for decades. Deftly, Glatzer constructs complex composites — often using select details to suggest the multifaceted character of these people and the paradoxes of their personalities. The ironies are abundant, and Glatzer's wry sense of humor is expressed through just the right whimsy when portraying a given situation (as often one of the "great ones" is seen in an all-too-human moment). In these portraits, life is comprised of high achievements mixed with odd moments, great minds and small-mindedness, the cultured and the quixotic. There is an aesthetic deftness to the lines drawn — a simplicity of detail and voice; and a combination of the concrete and abstract that gives the profiles a parabolic aura. The reader is constantly invited to ponder the peculiarities of worldliness and wisdom.

The final section presents a variety of experiences and expressions of faith, both personal and social in nature. In the social experiences, Glatzer participates in or observes various situations in which selfhood is overcome, and he reflects upon them. The events themselves, and particularly Glatzer's portrayal, become moments of religious psychology. The commentaries catch the dialectics and tensions of religious practice — capturing complicated mixtures of crudity and refined spirituality, loneliness and community, ecstasy and escape. Much here is suggested by patterns of gesture and ritual, not verbal formulations; and much is equally conveyed by concrete actions and not abstractions.

Concreteness and interaction are also features of the personal experiences and expressions of faith, but here only two persons are usually involved. Shared moments elicit dialogues, and these reflect primary theological moments. For Glatzer, as for Rosenzweig, his theological mentor, the world is transformed by speech and the realities brought into existence through it. This is the modality of "speech-thinking" advanced by Rosenzweig, in which the way one person addresses or relates to another affects the concreteness of their encounter and expresses fundamental commitments. In this realm of basic interpersonal communication, theological abstractions have no place.

Much has been written about the notion of speech-thinking, but here we have remarkable examples of it by one who participated in Rosenzweig's theological revolution. To be sure, this does not mean that the issues of faith expressed thereby are necessarily of the highest or most refined level. It only means that through direct answers or gestures, metaphysical and ethical commitments are conveyed. These expressions of Jewish patterns of faith are sometimes used by Glatzer to criticize certain types of religiosity or thoughtlessness; in other instances, they serve to convey spiritual profundity or authentic piety. The simplicity of these moments reveals much of Glatzer's theological orientation.

A poignant incident that occurred in the fifties on a trip to Europe is typical. Glatzer was about to cross a street, when suddenly he felt a little hand in his with its unspoken request for help. He understood that here was an expression of simple and direct trust, and responded faithfully. Glatzer guided the child to the other side of the street, after which he was left with his thoughts. It is moments like these, muses Glatzer, that redeem the world, leading it from isolation to wholeness, and from the terrors of selves who are not personally present to each other. In a suggestive hint, Glatzer indicates that he knows that the holy moment is not forever, and that it does not cancel out the reality of uncaring times. Both exist — in the realm of the interpersonal as in the sphere of nature — and wisdom must bind them together. Private letters from the 1960s express the same teaching. Glatzer deeply believed in the transforming power of theological action, but wasn't blind to evil and the silences of nature.[52] He wrote of the need to know both and to work at the ethical and sacred with all one's power, striving as we must against weighty odds.

It is just here that Rosenzweig's idea of a "remnant" comes in.[53] The always realistic but truly spiritual Glatzer spoke and wrote on several occasions that a people's worth does not lie in numbers but in quality of dedication and task.[54] From the Jewish side, the remnant requires a commitment to moral and spiritual ideals. The political developments in Israel during the 1970s saddened him greatly, and his diary entries silently ponder whether the Jewish people still has the moral will to survive or whether its teachings have been transmitted and its life lived — and one should simply recognize that greatness for what it was and had achieved.[55] Perhaps the dark pessimism of Glatzer's private thoughts contributed to his sense of an ever-shrinking remnant, but it never diminished the power of his public challenge to the modern Jew.

In later years Glatzer turned more and more inward to his own deepest truths and to the memories of those truths. He even remarked that he wished he could return to the religious practices of his youth, for there he was most truly real.[56] He did not fully do so, but spent his final times at his great wooden desk in Watertown, at work. To the end of his life, selfless scholarship remained a path of silent piety.

Perhaps Nahum Glatzer's silences were a burden to himself as much as and more than to all those who loved him well. But he bore them as a vow and a prayer — and in the nobility of that truth fulfilled his ideal of service. He died among loved ones in February 1990. His tombstone is inscribed with the same simple phrase chosen by Martin Buber and Franz Rosenzweig before him. *Va-ani tamid immakh*, "Yet I am always with You" (Psalm 73:23).

It was my great fortune to have known Professor Glatzer during my student days at Brandeis University, then as a colleague, and finally as a family friend. His life was inexpressably enriched by the love, care, and vitality of his wife Anne, whom he first met as a lively and lovely young student in Frankfurt, and whom we all came to know as a woman of dignity, energy, and loyalty. Their daughter Judith, the devoted executrix of his papers, was especially loved. Both women honored me beyond measure with the request that I look at the memoirs and, when an evaluation of them was formed, to help present them to a wider audience. Their help was readily given, with characteristic generosity and warmth. Anne Glatzer has since died, but had the pleasure of seeing the project take shape. She actively participated with observations on the materials and reflections on poems and photos in her keeping. Judith Wechsler has been a dear friend and colleague in this collaboration done in service to her father, whose presence was always before us. I am particularly grateful for her advice on many points.

The materials are virtually as Nahum Glatzer left them. Editing was limited to correcting clear scribal lapses and adjusting the mood or syntax of several phrases where Germanisms crept in. In addition, several redundancies were deleted; and in two instances names were omitted out of consideration for living persons. The ordering of the materials is the responsibility of the editors, as are the annotations, notes, and brief biographical and other clarifications.[57]

— Michael Fishbane

Notes

1. This phrase occurs in a diary entry by Kafka for October 15, 1921; see Franz Kafka, *Diaries: 1914–1923*, ed. Max Brod and trans. Martin Greenberg and Hannah Arendt (New York: Schocken Books, 1949), 193. Glatzer chose it as the title of the volume presenting the life of Kafka in the writer's own words. The book appeared as *I Am A Memory Come Alive: Autobiographical Writings by Franz Kafka*, ed. Nahum N. Glatzer (New York: Schocken Books, 1974); the diary entry is recorded there on p. 203.

2. Glatzer frequently invoked his father's piety and devotion. He made note of it in "What I Have Learned," *Jewish Heritage*, Summer/Fall 1975: 54, and extensively in the memoirs below. See p. 57.

3. See below, *Der Alter Melammed*.

4. See below, *Bodenbach*.

5. These materials are not in the Glatzer collection of the public archive at Brandeis University (established 1992), but in the personal possession of Professor Judith Wechsler, who brought them to my attention and generously allowed me to review them.

6. Glatzer found the Bergman essay in a collection in his father's library (see below, *Father's Library*); and an excerpt from it is copied out in one of his little anthologies.

7. The letter was written during a stay in Berlin, on the way to Frankfurt, and is in the possession of the family; the episode with Buber appears among the Profiles, in the section on Buber. There are slight discrepancies between the two compositions with respect to the exact sequence of events. The letter is dated 6 Elul 5680 (August 20, 1920).

8. See below, *Martin Buber, The First Meeting.*

9. See below, *Buber and Rosenzweig as Bible Translators.*

10. As observed by Franz Rosenzweig, in a letter to Gertrude Oppenheim (October 5, 1921), after attending High Holidays services at Nobel's synagogue. See Glatzer, *Franz Rosenzweig, His Life and Thought* (New York: Schocken Books, 1953), 104.

11. Cf. Rosenzweig's remark to Joseph Prager, regarding Nobel, that "the soul of a *great* Jew can accommodate many things. There is danger only for the little souls." Letter of January 22, 1922.

12. For this study circle and related matters, see R. Heuberger, "Orthodoxy Versus Reform: The Case of Rabbi Nehemiah Anton Nobel of Frankfurt a. Main," *Leo Baeck Institute Yearbook* 3 (1992): 45–58. Members of this group contributed to the volume *Gabe, Herrn Rabbiner Dr. Nobel zum Geburtstag dargebracht* (Frankfurt, 1922).

13. This is the term used by both Glatzer and Franz Rosenzweig. See Rosenzweig's note from autumn of 1919 in Glatzer's *Franz Rosenzweig*, 88. *Volkshochschule* was the common German designation for institutes of adult education. The correct technical term would be *Frankfurter Gesellschaft für jüdische Volksbildung*, which was founded in 1919 by Georg Salzberger. The *Gesellschaft* provided "Volksvorlesungen" (public lectures) and excursions to Jewish sites. When Rosenzweig became involved with the *Gesellschaft*, he transformed it completely and renamed it the *Freies Jüdisches Lehrhaus* in 1920.

14. There is much interesting material on the exchanges and procedures of the translation below, p. 89; see also Glatzer's later essay, "Aus der Zeit der Buber-Rosenzweig Bibelarbeit," *Mitteilungsblatt*, Tel Aviv, July 16, 1965, p. 5. Glatzer also wrote frequently on Buber as an interpreter of the Bible. See his "Darko shel Martin Buber be-Mikra," *Bitzaron* 38.6, June–July, 1958, and "Buber as an Interpreter of the Bible," in *The Philosophy of Martin Buber*, ed. P. A. Schlipp and M. Friedman, in *The Library of Living Philosophers*, vol. 12 (La Salle, Ill. and London: Open Court and University of Cambridge, 1967).

15. See M. Buber's *Briefwechsel aus sieben Jahrzehnten*, Band II: 1918–38, G. Schäder, ed. (Heidelberg: Lambert Schneider Verlag, 1973), 265. Glatzer refers to this matter in *Corpus Hasidicum*, in the section dealing with Buber.

16. See the invaluable account provided by Glatzer, "The Frankfort Lehrhaus," *Leo Baeck Institute Yearbook* I, 1956.

17. See Glatzer's full account of the event in the Profile of S. Y. Agnon, below.

18. See the account in Gershom Scholem, *From Berlin to Jerusalem. Memories of My Youth* (New York: Schocken Books, 1980), 93f.

19. See the letter of August 30, 1920, reproduced in translation in Glatzer's *Franz Rosenzweig*, 94–98, especially p. 97.

20. The principle of service and action is a cornerstone of several of the important essays of Rosenzweig (like "It is Time"; "Towards a Renaissance of Jewish Learning"; and "The Builders") published with an introduction by Glatzer under the title *On Jewish Learning* (New York: Schocken Books, 1955).

21. Glatzer highlights his father as first bearer of this ideal to him, in *Jewish Heritage*, 55. He poignantly remarks, upon being accepted by the University of Frankfurt, that he can now be "of service" (see below, *Examination for the Gifted*).

22. One of Glatzer's more beautiful essays is his account of Rosenzweig's last year, originally published in "Shenato ha-Aharonah shel Franz Rosenzweig," in *Aley Ayin* (The Salman Schocken Festschrift; Jerusalem: Schocken Books, 1952). It is reprinted in the Glatzer

collection *Essays in Jewish Thought* (University, Alabama: University of Alabama, 1978).

23. For an appreciation of the man, see Nahum N. Glatzer, "Professor Josef Horovitz," *Gedenkreden an der Bahre von J. H. Horovitz* (Frankfurt a. M., 1931).

24. Berlin: Lambert Schneider. A new edition was subsequently published by Schocken Verlag, Berlin, 1933.

25. Cf. Buber's later (1954) essay, "Prophecy, Apocalyptic, and the Historical Hour," reprinted in *On the Bible. 18 Studies by Martin Buber*, ed. Nahum N. Glatzer (New York: Schocken Books, 1968).

26. See the references (for 1922–25) found in the bibliography of Glatzer's writings, published in *Texts and Responses. Studies Presented to Nahum N. Glatzer on the Occasion of his Seventieth Birthday by his Students,* M. Fishbane and P. Flohr, eds. (Leiden: E. J. Brill, 1975).

27. Berlin: Schocken Verlag, 1931. The co-editorship in the original edition reads: *Mitgeteilt von Nahum Norbert Glatzer und Ludwig Strauss.*

28. The volume was entitled *In Time and Eternity: A Jewish Reader.*

29. Ibid., 14.

30. Köln: Hegner Bücherei.

31. See the account below, pp. 60–61.

32. Berlin: Bücherei des Schocken Verlags, 27.

33. Ibid., 42.

34. Ibid., 81–82.

35. March to December, 1935 (18 sayings); January to November, 1936 (25 sayings); and January to September, 1937 (14 sayings).

36. See the essay by Ernst Simon, "Jewish Adult Education in Nazi Germany as Spiritual Resistance," in *Leo Baeck Institute Yearbook* I (1956): 68–104.

37. See the extensive memoirs below, *Salman Schocken.* Glatzer wrote a tribute to Schocken, entitled "Salman Schocken. An Appreciation," *Jewish Publication Society Bookmark* 4.4 (December, 1957): 15; also "Salman Schocken-80 Jahre," *Aufbau*, October 25, 1957, pp. 13 and 18.

38. Subsequent editions inverted the phrases of the title.

39. *Hammer on the Rock*, 5.

40. *A Jewish Reader*, 14.

41. The reader may consult my remarks in "The Aggadah: Fragments of Delight," *Prooftexts* 13(1993): 181–90.

42. Cf. his trilogy, *The Rest is Commentary: A Source Book in Judaic Antiquity* (Beacon Texts in the Judaic Tradition, vol. I; Boston: Beacon Press, 1961); *Faith and Knowledge: The Jew in the Medieval World* (Beacon Texts in the Judaic Tradition, vol. II; Boston: Beacon Press, 1963); and *The Dynamics of Emancipation: The Jew in the Modern Age* (Beacon Texts in the Judaic Tradition, vol. III; Boston: Beacon Press, 1965).

43. Glatzer quotes a hint of Rosenzweig's radical change during the Yom Kippur services of 1913 in an letter from Rosenzweig to his mother, dated October 23, 1913 and reproduced in translation in *Franz Rosenzweig*, 27–28. The personal account was conveyed to Glatzer orally by Rosenzweig's mother, who felt close to Glatzer and often expressed motherly affection for him. An early version of the conversion was reported by Glatzer in "Franz Rosenzweig: The Story of a Conversion," in *Judaism* 1 (1952). This was a prepublication of the Introduction to *Franz Rosenzweig*. In the late 1960s this account was publicly challenged by Rosenzweig's son Raphael, among others, and caused personal pain to the scrupulous and faithful Glatzer. I was

then a young colleague and recall sitting in the seminar room of the Near Eastern and Judaic Studies Department before a faculty meeting just after the matter broke. Glatzer (as Chair) was sitting at the head of the table engaged in a quiet exchange with Professor Alexander Altmann, who concluded his own remarks more audibly with the view that the matter was altogether shameful and that he, Glatzer, should not respond, because "It is beneath your dignity."

44. See the opening remarks of Milton Himmelfarb in *Commentary*, August, 1966.

45. See *Parables and Paradoxes*, by Franz Kafka, ed. N. N. Glatzer (New York: Schocken Books, 1961); *Franz Kafka: The Complete Stories*, ed. Nahum Glatzer (New York: Schocken Books, 1971); and *I Am a Memory Come Alive: Autobiographical Writings of Franz Kafka*, presented by Nahum Glatzer (New York: Schocken Books, 1974). See also Glatzer's study, *The Loves of Franz Kafka* (New York: Schocken Books, 1986).

46. See the letter to Gertrud Oppenheim from May 25, 1927 in *Franz Rosenzweig*, 160.

47. See the letter of August 1, 1931 in G. Scholem, *Walter Benjamin. The Story of A Friendship* (New York: Schocken Books, 1981), 170.

48. First published in *Between East and West, Essays dedicated to the Memory of Bela Horo-witz*; ed. A. Altmann (London: East and West Library: 1958), it was reprinted in *Arguments and Doctrines*, ed. A. Cohen (New York: Harper and Row, 1970).

49. The theme was important to Glatzer, and he published rabbinic sources pertinent to the matter; see "Faith and Action," *Judaism* 17.1 (1968).

50. In addition to this piece, Glatzer wrote many other essays on the Book of Job. See "The Book of Job and its Interpreters," in *Biblical Motifs*, ed, A. Altmann (Brandeis Texts and Studies, 3; Cambridge, MA: Harvard University Press, 1966); "Knowest Thou? . . . Notes on the Book of Job," in *Studies in Rationalism, Judaism, Universalism in Memory of Leon Roth*, ed. R. Loewe (London: Routledge and Kegan Paul, 1966); "Baeck-Buber-Rosenzweig Reading the Book of Job" (Tenth Leo Baeck Memorial Lecture), Leo Baeck Institute (New York, 1966); and "The God of Job and the God of Abraham: On Some Talmudic-Midrashic Interpretations of the Book of Job," *Bulletin of the Institute of Jewish Studies*.

51. *Parables and Paradoxes*, 13, 15 (English; 12, 14, German).

52. The point comes to expression in a letter to his daughter Judith, then studying in Jerusalem, in a letter dated October 3, 1961 (thanks to Judith Wechsler for allowing me to read this letter).

53. See *The Star of Redemption* (New York: Holt, Reinhardt and Winston, 1971), III.3, pp. 404, 410.

54. See in *Jewish Heritage*, 54–55.

55. This theme is mentioned in a date book from the end of August, 1976 (courtesy of Judith Wechsler).

56. In a datebook dated March 29, 1972 (courtesy of Judith Wechsler) and in personal conversation.

57. It is with pleasure that I thank Dr. Katja Garloff, now of Reed College, for bibliographic and other assistance. She graciously agreed to prepare initial drafts of some of the entries that appear in the Glossary at the end of this volume. I am most grateful.

Glatzer, 1925

I
Memories

Birth

It was my father's decision that I be born and not die in my mother's womb. A physician had announced to mother that she would not be able to bear a child. She did conceive, but when the time of delivery drew near an affliction developed inside her; the surgeon determined that an operation was necessary, a move that would make the abortion of the child necessary. Mother reported — orally, later also in her memoir — that everything was prepared for the operation when father emphatically prohibited the surgery and the whole thing was called off, to the consternation of the medics. Father's motif was a religious one; he deeply believed that God wanted this child to be born and things cannot go wrong. Things went right. Birth took place, and mother recovered from whatever ailed her. Thus following medical wisdom (of the period), I had no chance to live; the simplicity of a father's faith gave me that chance.

My Grandfathers

My paternal grandfather, after whom I was named, was a keeper of the lands and forests of a big Polish or Ukrainian lord and bore the title (or designation) of *opszad dvorsky* (the precise meaning of which I do not know).* His father's name was Issakhar. The clan originated in Glatz, Silesia. The family lived in Janóvka, apparently not far from Buczacz (my father pronounced it Betshutsh), in a farmhouse; grandfather had to make daily rounds with a rifle, symbol of his office, in or around the lord's territory and, I guess, had to make regular reports. He was supposed to be a good swimmer. Once a week (or so) a teacher used to come from the city to instruct the children in Hebrew and, probably, in basic Polish or Ukrainian. The children were Jacob, the eldest; Gedaliah, my father, Sigmund, and

---

*Possibly Polish *obszar dworski*, meaning something like "the range or extent of the manor estate or courtyard."[1]

their sister Shayndel, who was later on called Charlotte. The grandfather was a proficient reader of the Torah. I suppose once a year, in the High Holiday period, he took his family, or at least, the male members, to the big city (Buczacz?); there he could practice the art of Torah reading.

My father told me that his father used to predict the future of the children. "You Dudye [David, my father's other Hebrew name] will become a blacksmith." And father used to add: "And am I less than a blacksmith?" Since his merchandise was hardware, he felt that his father's prediction was accurate.

Grandfather died in his younger years, after a swimming contest. Upon his death, the family moved to the city and grandmother (of whom I know nothing beyond her name, Dvorah, née Schwartz) opened a tavern (*kretshme*) for the peasants who used to come in for a drink or two after work or between shifts. This way she supported herself and the children until they were old enough to take care of themselves. My father accepted an apprenticeship at the merchant Rubin Leib Pohorille (if my memory is correct). He considered himself as a dweller of Buczacz (he was too young when the family left Janóvka) and told stories of Buczacz's scholars, saints, and men of good deeds – material which I found later in the works of S. Y. Agnon. I felt proud of Buczacz.

After finishing his apprenticeship (father had no formal education), he left Buczacz for Lemberg, the metropolis of Galicia, to make his way as a businessman in the area of hardware and farming equipment.

His engagement to my mother must have been arranged by friends. Her father was Osias Gottlieb, a hat manufacturer, who had a son (Leopold) and several daughters (Rachel, Jetty, my mother). His wife died young and the daughters were put in charge of the various business activities. My mother was thus trained in bookkeeping, correspondence, etc. She must have been an excellent student (my father used to poke fun at her grades of "excellent" all through). She read the classics of the time, went to the theater and to balls. My father had none of these interests.

From time to time, mother used to go out and visit her father and take me along. I remember the old man with his Kaiser Franz Joseph beard; he used to offer me cookies, which he kept in a metal box. Once in town, we visited mother's aunt Edna who lived alone and much enjoyed the visits, and aunt Diamond who owned a big grain store (and sat in the cashier's chair) and a movie house next to the store. As a relative I could enter without a ticket; I was too young to enjoy this "experience."

Once a year mother took me to the Lemberg Temple: on the eve of the Ninth of Ab, on which traveling was permitted. I remember the service: the rabbis, in clerical garb, sat next to each other at a table covered with a black cloth and each recited a chapter of Lamentations. The modern aspect was that they did not use the traditional chant, but straight, solemn, slow reading.

There are still in existence symbolic representations of my parents' marriage: the *tallit* that mother brought for father according to tradition; the *kittel* that she sewed for him, to be worn on the Days of Awe and at the Passover Seder; and a silver cup for *kiddush* and *havdalah*. They survived all our wanderings and we keep and use them lovingly. The cup is in constant use on Sabbaths and holidays, the *kittel* I wear when leading the morning services on the Days of Awe, the *tallit* (already quite brittle) we used at my and Anne's wedding (as a canopy), then at the weddings of Daniel and Nadya and Judith and Richard Wechsler. I hope it will be used as a shroud at my burial, together with father's *kittel*.

One Hundred and One

From my father's stories of his grandparental generation or the generation before. There was a woman, an aunt or grand aunt, exceedingly pious and God fearing. Her special merit was personally distributing food to poor families in the village, especially on Fridays, in preparation for the Sabbath; no one should go hungry on the holy day, or unable to observe the "three meals" according to age-old custom. She died a very old lady, in fact, one hundred and one years of age. Her last words were remembered: "Hundert und eins ist alles eines," i.e., at 101 all is one. By which she probably meant that there comes a time when life and death are no longer antagonists, cruel opposites, when living and dying are two aspects of the same process, when life becomes death, and death — life.

The Rebbe's Warning

My father used to tell the story of an uncle (or grandfather) whose name was Meir. This man, a businessman, is the only known hasid in our family. Before an important transaction he used to travel to his rebbe to get his opinion and advice. One day he appeared in the rebbe's court and related to the master the deal he was about to make. The rebbe thought for a moment, then declared: "Meirl, take off your coat." The winter was especially severe and the advice (or was it a command?) did not make sense. "What does the rebbe mean?" asked the bewildered hasid. "I mean what I say, take off your coat, Meirl." For the first time in his life, Meirl disbelieved the saintly advisor. He went, closed the deal, lost all his money—and his heavy warm winter coat, which the other side took in partial payment. Then Meirl understood what the rebbe meant. My father told the story in a tone of voice that indicated that he, the father, would have of course understood the cryptic warning.

Lemberg

Memories from Lemberg, up to 1914, when we left the city (outbreak of World War I): These memories crowd my mind; over and over again they present themselves. Perhaps the ghostlike images will vanish once they are written up on cold paper.

The Levaye

Not a funeral procession, but, indeed, a *levaye*, the accompanying of the dead. I was taking a walk, probably with the maid. A large group of Jews was approaching to my right, down below the street, in front of them a bier (or was it a black coffin?) of natural wood, covered with a black cloth? It occurred to me that they were walking so fast, as distinct from the Christian funeral processions that were slow, measured, dignified. I was informed that it is not proper for a dead Jewish person, especially for a pious man, to be driven by horses. So I appreciated that the body carried here by his fellow men must be one of a saintly Jew. And the fast walk is not a sign of disrespect but of an eagerness to observe a commandment (here the commandment of burying the dead) and to help the dead find his final rest as soon as possible.

Gal Ed

"Hill of Testimony"—a synagogue. I felt happy and proud to accompany my father to the prayers. My Hebrew teacher, Reb Leibush Shorr, prepared me for the singing of *yetziv pitgam*, the special Shavuot hymn.* I was to recite

*Recited on the second day of the Festival, before the prophetic lection

it in public, which I considered a high point in my young life. I do not remember whether I was asked to sing the piece, or whether Reb Leibush (who acted as the second or third cantor) was denied his request. But I still remember the melody. I never heard it again.

Once at election time the contenders for an office engaged in a heated debate in front of the ark. The debate grew more and more loud; my father stood not far away and said nothing (how could he have interfered?). I felt disgusted and ashamed that this sacred spot was used for a rather mundane purpose. The place should inspire awe, respect, silence. I learned an early lesson on human behavior in and out of holy places.

The Two Crowns

A dream. The Gal Ed synagogue, before people entered. On the *bimah* two Torah crowns were displayed, one big and beautiful, the other smaller and less ornate. I felt I had the choice between the two. I reached for the small crown and tried to place it on my head. It was too small and uncomfortable. I replaced it and was ready to take the bigger one; I could not reach it and wanted to use the stool under the *bimah*. In this moment a large crowd rushed into the synagogue. I did not dare reach for the crown and left the *bimah* in fear.

Dog Catchers

Their carriage stops. They come down, three of them with their loops. They take up positions so that the poor stray dog has no chance to escape. The dog tries to run in one direction. No use, one of the catchers is in his way. The dog, agitated, thinks of another corner; to no avail. Two or three steps and the dog ends up in one of the loops. He is being grabbed and put in the wagon. The men, silently, ascend and proceed. How symbolic of much in life.

Sin

I sensed very early—I guess this is natural—that there is something strangely "forbidden" in a boy's relationship to the other sex. A dark, indefinite, undefined, intuitive feeling; not more. One day, however, it must have been early in 1914, I accompanied father to a downtown bank, and waited outside while he went to the teller. I noticed a young girl, perhaps a bit older than I was; beautiful face, dark dress, fine movements. Suddenly I knew: this is it. Sin, forbidden lure that is to be resisted.

Dead Children

Quite often: A funeral officer, carrying a small white coffin on his right shoulder, followed by the child's parents. The latter resigned to their fate, sad, perhaps with a prayer in their heart. The officer, bored, used to his sorry task. The white coffin: for the child's soul is pure. One officer: The load is light. A short life.

I remember, street boys used to call (in Polish) to the undertakers in their uniforms returning from a funeral: "So and so, such and such, give the soul back!"

Beggars

Many of them, and quite often, came to the door, knocked softly (so that by the manner of the knocking you knew who it was) and humbly asked for a donation. I guess it was impossible to satisfy all who came. So again and again my mother refused, saying — if I recall correctly — *Pan Bóg oplaci*, the Lord God will pay. I felt like hiding so that the beggar's eye should not meet mine. How could the good Lord be charged with things that are clearly man's? The phrase must have been a common one but I was annoyed that it was my mother that used it.

Suicide

Suddenly: A man was carried on a stretcher in one of the court balconies; he tried to sit up and moved his upper body up and down, obviously in pain. Neighbors related that it was a student who tried to commit suicide. The unusual scene shocked me. Something terrible must have happened to him, I thought, but did not dare to inquire about what possibly only the victim knew and, possibly, not even he.

Flight

Beginning of World War I. The Russians advanced westward and stood before Lemberg. My parents were among those who decided to leave the city. Quickly they packed silver and small valuables into straw mattresses in their bedroom. They and the three children (Fanny was only three or four years old) with some hand luggage hurried to the railway station. The station was crowded with people waiting for a train going west, toward Vienna. We landed in a cattle car, packed with men, women and children. The train moved slowly and made long stops, but move it did and we were glad to be out of the danger zone. It was hot and people were thirsty. Suddenly a man called: "Who wants water?" Everybody shouted, "I do," to which the man replied: "Me too." There was laughter. It was on this journey that my father decided not to go to Vienna because of the corrupting influence of the big city (which he knew well from his travels) but to stop in Ungarisch Brod, Moravia, known for its Jewish community and Dr. Moses Jung's Jewish school. The information, however, was dated. Dr. Jung had some time ago moved to London to become rabbi of the Orthodox community. We remained in Brod anyway. It became clear that there wouldn't be a return to Lemberg to retrieve the valuables from the straw mattresses. Plans were made to move north, near the German border, so as to immigrate to Germany as soon as the war was over.

Ungarisch Brod

In Brod I came to know the way of life of a small, cohesive, secluded, premodern Jewish community: a valuable experience. I was attracted by the big synagogue, its rabbi, Dr. Klein (who always wore a top hat), its chief cantor, Herr Körner (with whose frail blond daughter, Teresa, I fell in love). I knew the chief slaughterer, Herr Katona, who impressed young and old by his magic tricks. His son, Erwin, was a dear friend. I used to watch Herr Katona skillfully slaughtering chickens and geese; I felt no pity for the tiny animals; after all, the slaughterer pronounced a benediction and performed a ritual according to the law. I liked best the small, intimate *klaus** and especially the Sabbath afternoon service. The Jewish school, headed by Herr Fischel, was a joy, especially after the severe gymnasium in Lemberg.

Dayyan** Weiss gave me instruction in Talmud. Study was often interrupted by serving maids rushing in with gasping geese who had to be slaughtered while alive to make them ritually acceptable; or by house-

---

*Study and prayer hall. **A judge or adjudicator in a rabbinic court

39

wives who presented an organ of a fowl for ritual examination. I admired the *dayyan*, who so quickly could pass judgment, positive or negative. It must have been May or June 1915 that we moved to Bodenbach an der Elbe, North Bohemia.

Bodenbach

1915–1920: Five years only; but in retrospect it appears like a much longer period. In it I grew to full consciousness. The war was going on; food was scarce and we were constantly hungry. Mother tried her best to produce tasty dishes out of the little that was available. Father served in the army (as a postal clerk, somewhere not at the front) and at times came home on leave. I dreaded these visits because in them the tenor of the house changed; nothing was ever right in his sight; one felt guilty and on the alert. War and the service broke up his business relationships and activities: there was very little money around. But father saw to it that we did not appear poor; there were higher and more important things in life: prayer, study, the Sabbath — the heritage of Israel. I was given the notion that it is up to me to preserve it, to teach it to others. The fact that I was the only boy in town (outside the refugee group) to engage in Hebrew studies, the only one in school to observe the Sabbath, did in no way give rise to the question as to who is right: I or "they." I had the truth and they were in error; of this I was convinced.

I assembled a small group of disciples whom I taught the *Sayings of the Fathers*: Karl Menzel (who died a young man), Joseph Soudek, Hugo and Ernst Insel, the cantor's sons, and my brother Bernhard. This study was more than an imparting of a translation of these bits of wisdom; it was an introduction into the thinking and the very life of our ancients. Later on, this attitude to the Hebrew classics grew stronger and deeper and determined my life.

We Jewishly interested youngsters formed an association called "Matteh Aaron" (Aaron's staff); Heinz Paechter, son of the president of the Bodenbach Jewish community, was the "chairman for religious affairs." We held worship services, organized a small circulating library of Judaica, and issued a handwritten bulletin with the members' contributions.

My own teachers in Hebraics were Herr Maisels and "der Alter Melammed."

Herr Maisels

He was a traditional *ḥumash* (Pentateuch) teacher who came from Eastern Europe on a refugee transport. My father engaged him to come, I believe, daily. He was tall, red-haired and smelled of hunger and poverty. The thumb of his right hand was always bandaged; he pretended to have a wound there which exempted him from army service. After all, you can't shoot if your right thumb does not cooperate. His method of teaching was to fuse the (Yiddish) translation of the text with as much rabbinic commentary as possible. Rashi, too, was studied; the scrolls in connection with the festivals; the Passover Haggadah; *akdamut** before Shavuot; the cantillation of Torah and Prophets; a *pshettl*** to be delivered at the Seder (it was on Tractate *Pesaḥim* 88), et cetera. I started to record the Pentateuch interpretations in small notebooks; I don't recall for what purpose; possibly just for the fun of writing.

Der Alter Melammed

His name was Herr Alter, a Talmud teacher by profession; so we called him "Der Alter Melammed." He lived with his two daughters in a one-room shed at the shore of the Elbe river in Tetschen. I went to him every weekday evening, equipped with a volume of *gemara****and a candle; there was no other light in the shed. "I am not your teacher," he said when we started; "Rashi is your teacher. Do you know why God created two hands? So that with the finger of one hand man can point to the text, and with the other to Rashi (printed on the margin of the text); so he will not feel lost." He was an old man with a long beard; one of his eyes was blind, the other seemed overly large. At certain nights he used to send his daughters out to draw water from a well, since "the well of Miriam makes its rounds."[2] A strange kind of reality in which a Jew moves. Often I got tired, after the long hours at school, homework in the afternoon and now these studies. Then he used to say: "The candle wants to burn and you don't want to study." For a while I really believed in a candle's dedication to the sacred task.

*Medieval poem in Aramaic, recited before reading of the Torah on first day of the Festival.
**A brief clarification. ***Explicatory section of the Talmud

Teachers of Hebrew

None was good enough from my father's viewpoint. They were changed quite often; I remember only Reb Leibish Schorr. One even tried on me the modern "Hebrew in Hebrew" method. He did not last, for all was speech, and not much material. Material, Pentateuch, that is, was the chief purpose of study. At a point, father was sure I could pass an informal exam, administered by a friend of father's on his way back from the synagogue. I don't remember what I did right, only the verse that stopped me: "Look down from Thy holy abode, from heaven." I felt much ashamed and ignorant.

The Scholar's Abode

Most probably upon my father's suggestion, I went to visit a man supposedly of great learning, a refugee. I found myself in an almost empty room. The man was sitting at his desk and told me that he was writing a book; it must have been within the context of tradition, a Talmudic or biblical commentary, or a commentary on a commentary. I was struck by the contrast of his barely maintained external life and the spiritual dedication. Another sign and symbol of Judaism as I came to know it in those early years.

Father's Library

His library consisted of only a few books: two prayer books (a big one for general use, and a small one, for his travels); a Festival Prayerbook and *ma'amadot*, readings for every day of the week, I think, cut out from the big Siddur, for he recited them every day and wanted to have the collection when on travels; a *Tikkun Lel Shavuot*, Vienna 1869, readings culled from Hebrew classical literature, to be recited on the night of the Feast of Weeks when the pious stay awake in preparation for celebrating the revelation on Mt. Sinai; finally, a Hebrew-German edition of *Hovot ha-Levavot* (Duties of the Heart) by the eleventh-century Baḥya ibn Pakuda of Saragossa. The work, written in Arabic and translated into Hebrew, offers the first well-organized presentation of Jewish ethics. The author stressed humility, trust in God, love of God, and study of philosophy as the "duties of the heart," in contradiction to the external religious duties performed by the limbs. Under the influence of Moslem Sufism, Bahya counsels a mildly ascetic way of life. My father loved this work and studied it many times. While still in Lemberg, he engaged a teacher to study the book with him. Later, in Bodenbach, he perused the *Duties* by himself and introduced me to the work. It was important to him that here a Jew wrote in Arabic a book in which classical Judaism (Bible, Talmud) lived in harmony with Islamic Sufism.

In 1918, after the death of the Bodenbach rabbi, Max Freund, father bought from the rabbi's family a set of the Babylonian Talmud, Prague 1830, and the Mendelssohn edition of the Bible with the *Biur*. Outside the set of the Talmud there was a tractate, *Niddah*, Vienna 1845, which an Austrian officer, a resident of Bodenbach, sent to the rabbi during the (First) War. In the dedication the donor noted that he found the tractate on the Russian battlefield. Most probably, a Jew, fleeing from the enemy, carried the volume as his treasured possession until it became too heavy a burden, or even more probably, until he was felled by a soldier's bullet. The officer's Jewish heart made him go to the trouble to pick up the sacred volume and carry it to the next camp to be shipped to his rabbi.

Another Talmudic volume was inscribed by a refugee Talmudist, who expressed his gratitude to the rabbi for allowing him to use that volume. I, too, got permission to study Talmud from one or another of these tomes. But now, the whole set was my father's, and by extension, mine.

In 1918 my father bought a copy of *Das Buch vom Judentum*, published by the Bar-Kochba Society in Prague 1913. Here I saw for the first time an attempt to blend inherited Judaism with the modern spirit. Gustav Landauer wrote "Sind das Ketzer-Gedanken?" The very title intrigued me. So, it was possible to be a heretic within the wider concept of Judaism. The volume concluded with translations from the Zohar; a fascinating new world. Of great impression was Hugo Bergman's essay "Kiddusch Haschem," in which he explored the Judaic view of the "Sanctification of the [Divine] Name" which, ultimately, means martyrdom. With a wide sweep, Bergman connected antiquity with the present day and concluded with the words, "Zionismus ist unser Kiddusch Haschem," Zionism is our way to sanctify the name of God. At once Zionism assumed a previously undetected perspective, and *kiddush hashem* could find expression in a modern Jewish movement. The articles were by no means profound; what mattered to me then was the novel perspective.

Birthday presents for Bernhard included a beautifully published

Scholem Asch's *Kleine Geschichten aus der Bibel*, translated from the Yiddish, and a German translation and commentary on the Pentateuch by Julius Fürst, with reproductions of zoo etchings by Gustave Doré (Prague, no date).

The volume *Sippurim*, published in Prague (originally in 1853), was a collection of Jewish stories, biographies and memoirs from olden times. Evenings, Mother used to read the stories to us during the war, and I felt always proud to belong to the people that was alive in these stories.

At the Gymnasium we used the presentation of Jewish history by Kaiserling-Biach-Doctor, which gave me some historical orientation; the accompanying anthology was uninspiring and outright boring. Heinrich Graetz's *Popular Jewish History* (*Volkstümliche Jüdische Geschichte*), in three volumes, was full of life, movement, and some depth; I read in it with much inner participation and used it in preparation for the course in Jewish history that I gave to the little group of youngsters in Bodenbach.

Father entered for me a subscription for *Jung Juda,* a youth periodical that appeared in Prague. It was Zionist, historical, cultural, mildly religious. I had written an essay, "Scholar," in the religious-romantic-aggadic vein and sent it to *Jung Juda* in the hope they would publish it. That was in 1918 and would have been my first appearance in public. It came back with the editor's note, "Nice but not publishable." He was damn right.

A weekly Jewish periodical *Oesterreichische Wochenschrift*, edited by Joseph Bloch, was devoted to problems of the day, Jewish rights, anti-Semitism, Zionist activities, and brought reports of Jewish life all over the world. All these publications contributed to a widening of the horizon, helped to deepen my commitment to Judaism, and counteracted the defamation and humiliation I experienced at the Gymnasium.

Special pleasure came from reading in the Mendelssohn Bible, mentioned before. The very layout of the page, the good paper and superior print added to the joy gained from the text itself.

Mother inherited from her father several volumes of Goethe and Heine, parts of the 150-volume edition of classical literature (*Meyers Klassiker Ausgaben*). I loved to read Goethe poems and some of them I learned by heart. Heine was an exhilarating experience. Naturally I concentrated on "Hebräische Melodien" and was proud of Heine's ties to Judaism. But the free flow of his poetry, the right touch and measure of criticism also appealed to me and expressed at least one part of my relationship to the world.

The Talmud and Mendelssohn Bible, the *Tikkun* and *Ḥovot ha-Levavot*, the little Prayerbook, the *ma'amadot*, and the Goethe and Heine volumes are still with me (1978). Whatever will be the fate of my own library when I am gone, I hope the *Ḥovot ha-Levavot* and possibly the little prayer book will remain in the family, at least for one more generation. I do not dare to hope beyond these twenty or thirty years.

The Ninth of Av

In 1920 I wrote a deeply felt sketch "The Ninth of Av" and mailed it to *Jung Juda*. It appeared under the main title "From the Circle of our Readers."[3] That was my first appearance in print. Seen from any later perspective, the article was childish and of possible meaning only to myself at the time. However, the theme of destruction, despair, hope, reconstruction kept on appearing in my thought with ever greater force.

Yiddish Songs

Hugo Insel, no doubt taught by his father, sang Yiddish songs of which I remember "A Millner's Treren," the milliner's tears. I shed tears because "di reder dreien sich, di yuren gaien sich," the wheels turn and the years go by. The songs were sentimental, elegiac, pious. Of deep impression were *Die Lieder des Ghetto* by Morris Rosenfeld, which appeared in German translation, sumptuously published (Berlin, 1902). I read them many times and knew some of them by heart: the outcries of social injustice and the sad, sad depictions of Jewish religious life. The tragic note seemed to me all-pervasive in our heritage; it rang true.

I decided — supported by father — to become a rabbi and to use this office as a vehicle for whatever I would have to say. The rabbi of Bodenbach, Max Freund, influenced me indirectly. I used to criticize his views of religion and he, in turn, considered me a zealot (which in a way I was). He must have been really angry, for one Friday evening he preached a sermon against me, in effect excommunicating me and applying to me a biblical text on a leper: "Alone shall he dwell, outside of the camp is his dwelling place." He could have known that such a procedure would only increase my determination to propagate my brand of Judaism. Soon after that sermon he died.

Gymnasium

The exact name of the school was Kaiser-Königliches Staats-Oberreal-Gymnasium in Tetschen. It offered courses for humanists (eight years Latin, six years Greek), semi-humanists (less Latin, no Greek, a foreign language, more natural science), and "realists" (no classics, more languages, math and sciences). My choice was the humanist course. Greek was taught by the sadist and mostly drunk Professor Schwab (who later died of alcoholism), the other subjects by other unpleasant characters. German literature was to me the most attractive subject; the least attractive was gymnastics, taught by Professor Vogt, who ridiculed me for my clumsiness: I was not even able to climb a dangling rope. The zoologist called upon me whenever his anti-Jewish heart dictated; I was supposed to be an expert on lice, bed-bugs, and such. The classmates were mostly anti-Jewish; and since there was only one other Jew in class (Feigl) and he tried to belong to the others, anti-Jewish meant primarily anti-Glatzer. As my German was imperfect and my behavior a bit outlandish, I was an easy target for ridicule. My bench-mate was Olaf Jordan, a friendly, witty fellow, who did not accept the class's verdict of me; friendly, too, was Ingeborg Stolterfoot, who lived in the neighborhood of our home (Schäferwand-Strasse 7 — up the hill) and with whom I often took the way home. On Sabbaths my sister Fanny had — on father's command — to carry books for me; I disliked both the idea and the practice; to her it gave a strange notion of Jewish observance and of the role of women in Judaism.

1918–1919

The war ended; Germany and Austria lost abominably; famine continued; various parties propagandized their respective cause and held rallies on the Schäferwand; there was much excited oratory. Allenby conquered Palestine, which thus ceased to be part of the Turkish Empire. At home there was much talk of our family's settling in Palestine; I was looking forward to it with deep longing; the symbolism of a child returning to his mother was much on my mind. But the original plan to move to Germany — at least for a time — seemed more practical. Perhaps my education was foremost in my father's thinking in deciding in favor of Germany. About August 1920 he took me to Berlin. After a half-hearted attempt to place me there, we continued (after the High Holidays) to Frankfurt; he had already corresponded with the Breuer Yeshivah and a family where I could have room and board.

Frankfurt am Main, 1920–21 and Later

I was accepted as a student (*bakhur*) at Rabbi Solomon Breuer's Yeshivah. Room and board was with Frau Johanna Schott, Rückerstrasse. Rabbi Breuer gave the main lecture ("Haupt-Shiur") daily at 11 a.m. The discourse was far too advanced for most of us; but the main evil was that the old man's voice was barely audible; we crowded around his stand but even this did not help much. The course in preparation of the "Haupt-Shiur" was given by lesser lights. The whole idea was to reach the state of self-study, to have command of major parts of certain tractates, and to study the codes on the side until one was ready to pass the big examination, qualifying for *semikhah*:* a most unsystematic, unorganized "curriculum." We students were of course conscious of the fact that Breuer was the son-in-law of the great Samson Raphael Hirsch, and the young Breuers were Hirsch's grandsons. The separatist-Orthodox and anti-Zionist ideology of the Agudat Yisrael movement was expected to be adhered to by the students, and most did follow the unwritten rule. Here our ways parted. I was a Zionist and my outlook, though strictly observant, rejected Hirsch's and Breuer's separatism. The fact that I secretly attended the Talmud study group of Rabbi N. A. Nobel came out. Dr. Isaac Breuer, the lawyer who took part in the affairs of the Yeshivah, called me to his home and in a speech combining hostility, sarcasm, and sanctimoniousness, tried to persuade me to break with Nobel, repent, and attach myself fully to the Breuer philosophy. I enjoyed the oratory and that he so much cared about the salvation of my soul. My answer was a clear No.[4] I left the Yeshivah.

Freedom

Relieved of the constraints of the Yeshivah and of the parental environment, I felt a sense of sweet freedom. I could organize my day as I wanted, read and study what attracted me, dream of becoming a writer and public

*Rabbinical ordination

lecturer. I had a seat in the Stadtbibliothek and ordered books and periodicals. I enrolled as a non-registered student at the University and took courses in Semitic studies, philosophy, classics. I gave private lessons and taught courses in the Religionschule, later at the [Freies Jüdisches] Lehrhaus and the Pädogogische Akademie, in the latter as a substitute for Rabbi Jacob Horovitz. I wrote articles for the local *Mitteilungsblatt* of the Jewish Youth organizations in Frankfurt. Of course I felt I had to formalize my education, pass the external high school exams, and become a full-time student at the University. This I postponed from semester to semester. More important to me was to live in freedom. I enjoyed the beauty, charm and intelligence of some of young ladies and the dedication, industry and sense of purpose of men my age and older: Fritz Goitein, Ernst Simon, Erich Fromm, Erich Itor Kahn, Josef Soudek, Moshe Silberg. I lived frugally and saved every penny possible. Twice a year, for Passover and the High Holidays, I went to Elberfeld, where my parents had moved from Bodenbach. My father still hoped I would become a rabbi and only slowly, reluctantly I convinced him that scholarship was dearer to me. I could not possibly give him a full account of my life. His relationship with mother had improved. For years he avoided talking to her and when he did he used the third person or the impersonal German "Mann." The change was visibly indicated by my mother expecting a baby. Dvorah (Resi) was born in the night after Yom Kippur 1921 and the child brought light and joy into the austere and usually sad home. Father, who never showed much concern for my sister Fanny, was in love with Resilein. Economically: after father's initial success as partner in a tool factory, things again started to look dim and the family talked about immigration to Palestine. I was to finish my studies and follow them. Every time after visiting Elberfeld it was good to be in my beloved Frankfurt again.

Sex Education

Du schonst Dich nicht! You ruin yourself. I knew that something highly unpleasant will follow when my father thus addressed me. He had noticed marks of a nocturnal emission and came to warn me of the seriousness of the situation. These are, he maintained, early signs of a venereal disease which ruins body and soul. I was shattered. I knew that something was wrong; perhaps some erotic thoughts at daytime led to erotic dreams and to emissions. But I could not imagine that it was worse than this. On the other hand, I could not disbelieve my father. I promised to be more cautious with my emotional life. And very piously I read the prayers for forgiveness, ordained for such occasions.

A sequel to this. Later, in Frankfurt, I felt pain in the calf of the right leg and consulted Dr. Richard Koch. He asked: "Did you ever suspect you had a venereal disease?" I admitted that indeed I had. I was terribly frightened. I don't remember what his medical wisdom prescribed. But the pain continued and one day I had a checkup with Dr. Leon Marx and I brought up the problem of this strange pain. He looked at my legs and feet and pronounced: "My boy, you have flat feet. You need supports." I got supports; the pain ceased. Thus ended the chapter of that horrid disease. But, naturally, my sex education was far from completed.

The Young Ladies

There was Bettina, a student of piano and voice, vivacious, intelligent, charming. I used to visit her and listen to her music, have good talks and then have tea with her and her parents. The parents were kind to me and probably hoped I would propose. That was out of the question; I wanted sometime to establish a Jewish home, where the traditions of Judaism were kept alive and children raised to be a part of the people of Israel. But even this friendly relationship came to an end when one day I discovered (in a volume she lent me) a letter by Abrasha (later Alexander) Schneider, where this lover inquired about the well being of his beloved Betyushka and expressed his hope to see her soon. That, of course, ended our friendship.

Maria was the most beautiful young woman far and wide. Betty introduced me to her. She took a dance class and belonged to a fashionable photographic atelier. I knew that she had other friends; all of her father's assistants (her father was a professor of psychiatry at the Frankfurt University) wooed her. Still, we were good friends. What fascinated me was the deep, deep beauty of her face and the graciousness of her presence. After a number of years she implored me to marry her. She intended to get a divorce from her husband (a professor of art history, a successor of Nietzsche and Jacob Burkhart) and expected me to dissolve my marriage. This ended chapter Maria.

At the time I did not realize that Erika, whom I tutored in Hebrew, was "interested" in me and hoped I would notice it and a serious friendship would develop. She took a course in Akkadian (not her field) in which I was enrolled and in class wrote me short notes in Akkadian. Still I did not notice that these were love letters. After a number of years, in Chicago, she revealed her heart.

I knew Anny (Anne) when she was a little girl with long braids. The decisive turn came when, in 1927, her parents went on a journey and asked me to keep an eye on Anny. The girl was lovely, always happy and fun-loving. I enjoyed her company and she found it interesting that I was not a zealot, traditional in my Jewish attitudes but not Orthodox. I guess she liked to be appreciated and paid attention to. I taught her some "advanced" Hebrew; I think our texts were poems by Judah ha-Levi. At one point I asked: "Do you understand this?" "No," she replied, "explain it with a kiss." I liked this fresh, direct, uninhibited approach. I do not remember the scene, but I am sure I "explained" the line in question to her satisfaction.

Her parents (Solomon and Bertha Stiebel) invited me often to Sabbath and Holiday dinners. Her father was a business man, partner with the firm Butonia, and a Zionist highly respected in the Jewish community; intelligent, erudite in certain fields, (e.g., history of Britain), of wise judgment; a dominating character, yet of warm emotionality. Anne's mother came from a prominent clan (Fränkel, Bodenheimer, Feuchtwanger) and was of aristocratic bearing. I enjoyed the evenings at the Stiebels, talks with Solomon Stiebel and the lovely presence of Anne. An older brother was Walter (later, a student of medicine; in the Hitler period he was "captured" in a sanatorium and put to death) and a younger brother, Richard, who later succeeded his father in the business.

On one of our walks, Anne said spontaneously: "I would like to have a child with you." (There was no sexual background for this wish.) This sudden, of course unprovoked, utterance, surprised me and made me happy. As nothing else, it expressed her loving attitude to me. At that moment I felt most deeply that she should become the mother of my children. From then on our relationship became more intense and intimate. The parents were not sure whether their daughter made the right choice. After all, I was still a student; though I earned my livelihood by teaching and tutoring I had no firm position; I had no family nearby; the fact that I was an Östjude was no help either. Yet the Stiebels did not try to prevent the friendship with Anne to develop into an engagement and marriage.

Fall 1930 I had an "official" talk with Anne's father. That I had the sum of eight thousand marks in my bank account, convinced him that I was able to establish myself and found a family; he loved his daughter dearly and, naturally, wanted the best for her. Marriage, however, should take place once I have my doctoral degree.

Our engagement was celebrated in the fall of 1931. I was ceremoniously called to the Torah in the synagogue Friedberger Anlage. The marriage took place January 30, 1932, in the Stiebel home; Rabbi Jacob Horovitz performed the ritual;[5] Rafael Rosenzweig carried the bride's train. When after the ceremony the couple, according to custom, withdrew into an adjoining room, he refused to leave us alone. We excluded most family, for I had no family attending. Mrs. Adele Rosenzweig came from Cassel; Edith Rosenzweig was there, also Erich and Frieda Kahn,[6] Ernst and Bertel Mayer, Seff and Gretel Soudek, possibly the Pollacks and Fränkels.

Josef, the Butonia handyman, helped us to the railway station; we stopped for the night in Karlsruhe; next morning we saw in the papers the announcement of our marriage. On to St. Moritz and then via Venice to the land of Israel.

Examination for the Gifted

In 1920, i.e. shortly after the War, father was eager to move to Germany: for him to prepare for the aliyah to the land of Israel, for me to start rabbinical studies in Frankfurt. That I had not finished gymnasium did not bother him; I could, he thought, easily make up for it by a so-called "external" examination which would allow me to give more of my time to Talmud and commentaries – this too in preparation for Palestine.

It was not that easy. I entered the Yeshivah of Rabbi Solomon Breuer, enrolled as a "guest student" at the University, and took courses in Philosophy and Semitics, became active in the Blau-Weiss movement (as a "leader" in one of the groups), started to give private tutorials and public lectures, became a lecturer at the Lehrhaus, fell in love, and started to write, especially for the *Frankfurter Jüdische Wochenzeitung*. The external examination, for which I kept studying, was several times postponed. My parents started to urge me: When, oh when? and I consoled them by giving the next possible date. I knew, of course, that one day I would have to undergo the ordeal.

Suddenly the Prussian Ministry of Culture issued an order that "especially gifted" (*ausserordentlich begabte*) students who for whatever reason did not finish their gymnasium studies could present themselves for a special examination in Berlin, which if successfully passed, would be the equivalent of a regular "Abiturium," i.e. the concluding examinations. Franz Rosenzweig applied for me and collected some recommendations on my behalf. I did not feel that I deserved all that attention but there was no way out.

I wrote to Frau Adele Rosenzweig, Franz's mother and very friendly in her attitude to me, that I was in love with a most lovely woman, Orientalia, and would soon go to Berlin, see her parents, and decide whether or not we shall enter marriage. If the family decides not to accept me, we would remain good friends though our relationship would be illegitimate in the eyes of the world.

Franz Rosenzweig did not catch the symbolism and thought Orientalia was a real person (though the name was a bit unusual). She, Frau Rosenzweig that is, answered immediately that she was surprised and did not expect "such a thing" from her great-grandson. (Since the title "grandson" was preempted by Rafael, I was made to be her great-grandson and she my great-grandmother, or *Uroma* in German.) I did not want her to be ashamed of me and replied by return mail. She was relieved.

The special exam was preceded by submission of previously done scholarly papers. I had done work on Babylonian mythology and submitted this material. My stuff was reviewed by Professor Eugen Mittwoch and graciously accepted. The journey to Berlin was filled with unusual anxiety; more and more I doubted whether I would be able to satisfy the professors, for it was they who administered the proceedings. In the morning there was a written exam, consisting of some scholarly essay questions, and in the afternoon the oral confrontation. A small group of us — not more than eight — waited in an anteroom in the Ministry and one by one we were called in. Each returned with a downcast face, to be informed after a short conference of the examiners that he had failed. I was the last one to be called in and saw no hope to be better off than the others. If I am not mistaken, the Minister C. H. Becker was among the examiners; the main questions were asked by Professor Ernst Sellin; one of them concerned the institution of the calendar in antiquity.

They gave me a sign to leave. I waited until called in again. A terrible feeling of failure, futility, and a messed-up life. In entering I was aware of the long distance between the waiting room and the end of the conference room where "they" sat. They told me that I passed my exam; congratulations. I was happy as never before in my life. Now the gate was open; now surely opportunities will present themselves and I shall be able to be of service, to do my part in academic life. On toward the doctorate.

On the way back to Frankfurt, I stopped in Cassel, to visit Mrs. Rosenzweig, to receive her good wishes and to be "spoiled" for a day or two. Fräulein von Kästner, who lived with Mrs. Rosenzweig, took me to the side and, in a grandmotherly fashion, admonished me not to allow this success to go into my head, but to remain modest, reticent, even humble. I accepted the admonition in gratitude.

At Court, Frankfurt am Main

For some time I was delegated by Rabbi Jacob Horovitz to act as Hebrew and Yiddish interpreter at the District Court in Frankfurt. I remember two episodes. A man was caught stealing a bicycle. While the investigation was going on the police intercepted a letter to him; it came from Paris and was what the court assumed to be in Hebrew. I was called in to translate the letter. The court officer instructed me to watch for clues that the letter may have come from an international organization of bicycle thieves.

My report was disappointing to the judge. The letter, in Yiddish, was written by the thief's mother in Paris. She had heard of her son's misdeed and of his involvement with the police. She expressed her sorrow and pain. She reminded him that upon his leaving home she had admonished him to be upright and honest. Now her son brings but disgrace on her and the whole family. She advised him to accept the judge's verdict, be it jail or a fine, repent and start a new life again. The judge realized that instead of an international criminal organization, he saw a Jewish mother pleading with her son to be "a Mentsch." It may well be that the court let him go free or imposed on him only a small fine.

The other episode concerned a man who was accused of writing obscene letters to the wife of the *dayyan* of the community. The man denied the accusation, but the court had evidence that the accusation was well founded. When the man was brought into the courtroom, I recognized him as the person I had long ago tutored in preparation for his conversion to Judaism. I was surprised that this man, whom I had known as gentle, reticent, correct and well intentioned, should be identical with the one accused of lewd, utterly despicable behavior. It was established that he had no contact with the *dayyan*'s wife, neither did he have any dealings with the *dayyan*. I felt that, maybe, the accusation was based on an error, and I should let the judge know my suspicion. I asked the court to be allowed to be heard as a witness. The request was granted and I declared that the man was, a few years ago, known to me as a decent human being, and I could not believe that he was the writer of the obscene letters. The judge did not find my testimony convincing and dismissed it. The man was found guilty, and I realized that my declaration was naive. Human nature is more complicated than I presumed at the time.

Wedding in Galilee

During my first trip to what was then Palestine (1927), I went to visit a Frankfurt friend named Rosenthal at his farm in Afula. He welcomed my coming, also, because I could accompany him to Yavneh, where — tomorrow — he would marry his chosen one. I was glad, because now my visit would serve a friendly purpose.

The following morning I awoke to see two horses, saddled and loaded with sacks of nuts and cookies, ready for a journey. My friend noticed my amazement and explained that the second horse was for me. After the wedding I should — as planned — continue my trip in the Galilee and his bride will use the horse for their trip to their newly established home in Afula. I protested that I never rode a horse and had not the faintest notion how to handle the animal. Never mind, said my friend; I'll help you to mount the horse, the rest is simple; hold on to the reins, pull the right if you want to turn right, pull the left if you want to turn left. Take it easy.

I had no choice. Once up on the horse I noticed the unexpected distance from the ground, which scared me a bit. Also the "sitting" was quite uncomfortable, since the "saddle" turned out to be the sack with the nuts and cookies, leaving very little space for the rider.

The journey went up the Emek valley. The scenery was most beautiful — once this was swamp territory, infested with malaria and poisonous flies. I had to watch my horse and could not pay too close attention to the

54

surroundings. One thing, however, my friend found he had to point out to me: to the right was one of the caves where "the witch of Endor" lived. (The witch consulted by King Saul, who defended the country against the Philistines and wanted to receive the blessing of the prophet Samuel, long dead; Saul fell in that war, he and two of his sons). The story always fascinated me, so for a few minutes I forgot my problem with the horse. Not for long, though. My horse was thirsty and whenever we passed a brook, he (or she) bent his (or her) head to get a drink. I was about to fall over and must have, unintentionally, pulled the reins which the horse understood to mean he (or she) should gallop. Of course, that was not my intention. At the next brook I was more careful. But now what I needed was a short rest for my legs, and I asked my friend to interrupt the ride. Under no circumstances, said my friend. Once you come down, you will not make it up the horse again. Don't worry, you will make it all right.

Somehow we made it. Upon arrival in Yavneh I was given a bed to stretch out in. I fell sound asleep and must have slept for hours. Suddenly I was awakened: Get up, the wedding is going to start. I felt rested and ready for the event. The yard in front (or the back) of the farmhouse was all prepared, the tables full of good things. The local youth was assembled and in a jolly mood. We heard the singing voices of the gang of young farmers coming from the neighboring villages. The old rabbi came and the brief ceremony took place in the open.

I had a good night's sleep. Next morning I said shalom to everybody, gave my horse a friendly look, and with my rucksack continued my journey until I reached the Jordan river and Tiberias. The Jordan was a surprise: famous in psalm, prayer, song, and miracle stories, it is but an unseemly little river. Again a fitting symbol of Israel: so little geography for so much history and legend.

Father's Death

August 1929. The papers were full of references to the Arab-Jewish conflict, of Jewish complaints of Arab provocations, of Arab accusations of Jewish misdeeds at the Western Wall. Extremists used big words and the British did not seem to care enough to interfere; they let things take their course.

At the time I was in Cassel, enjoying a vacation at Mrs. Adele Rosenzweig's beautiful home. A cable came from Tel Aviv:"Vater leicht vernrin-det," which must have meant: *verwundet* (injured). He was recovering from a cold (I think) in the home of the Makleff family in Moza, near Jerusalem. I hurried back to Frankfurt, after sending off a cable to mother: father should receive the best of care and I'll take care of the expenses. I feared the worst, perhaps "slightly injured" was what they told mother, or what they wanted me to believe. Soon came a second cable informing me of fa-ther's death in Moza on the eighteenth of Av, which was a Sabbath. I imme-diately started the seven days of mourning period (*shivah*). Ernst Neben-zahl, a law student at the time, came to help me do what had to be done, the tearing of the garment, the benediction praising God as "the true judge." That was a great help for I was bewildered in my sadness and needed a human being near me.

The details came in: The Arabs in Kolonye opposite Moza concluded a pact with the Jewish settlers in Moza (represented by Mr. Broze) that they will not attack. Broze is supposed to have asked father to move to his, Broze's, house until the storms blew over. Father refused in order to be help-ful to Makleff's children. Saturday afternoon, the Kolonye Arabs stormed down their hills and attacked the first house in Moza: Makleff's. Father di-rected one or two of the children to jump through the window to reach Broze's house and escape. The rest (the Makleffs, father, and a rabbi who was another guest there) hid under the beds. The Arabs attacked with knives and daggers, set fire to the house and escaped. The burial took place on Sunday; none of my family could be present. The graves were marked; later, a stone was placed there with an inscription which I sent in, using Judah ha-Levi's lines:

be-tzeti liqratkha
*liqrati metzatikha**

I bought the burial space next to father's; it was marked with my name. I visited the grave in summer 1977, on the Yahrzeit day, with Anne and Fanny. Later, in spring 1980, with Anne and Judy I read some psalms.

On the Friday night during the *shivah* period I went to the Hermes Weg synagogue. According to tradition I waited in the anteroom until the can-tor came to escort me in for the *kaddish*. All week many people from the

*When I went out towards You/I found You coming towards me[7]

56

community came to visit me. When Rabbi Jacob Hofmann entered, I stood up, but he motioned me to remain sitting. When Anne came, we decided to name our first child, if it should be a son, Daniel, in memory of my father.

Rosenzweig was deeply moved when I came to see him; and he wept.

———

All the time I asked myself whether this death has meaning. Much much later, after many years, I realized that death can be utterly meaningless.

It is not only in my dream-life that father did not die. He appears, older than he was in 1929, but takes part in my life, asks questions, but mainly is present in the full sense of the word. In my waking life he is far from dead. I hear him saying his prayers, singing the Sabbath hymns, donning the prayer shawl, putting on his phylacteries, walking next to me silently. Certain scenes from my childhood come to life, nothing unusual, just everyday things. So his life extends beyond his mortal days. There is significance in the Hebrew date of his death: *yod-ḥet* [18th day in the month of] Av or *ḥay** [i.e., *ḥet-yod*] *aʏ*. Father lives.

Dream

I make my way over snow and icy roads and enter a prayer room. In the corner sits my father, but I barely see him. I realize that I forgot my *tefillin* at home. Should I go back, though the road is steep and icy? I decide to go back and fetch the *tefillin*. I return, put them on, but do not enter the prayer room; I remain in the anteroom and say my prayers.[8]

Towards Hitler's Germany

From the mid-twenties on, I had the strange feeling that Germany is moving toward a radical change. The growth of the Nazi party and increasingly harsh voice of its leaders, especially of Hitler himself, made me feel more and more uneasy. I talked to my colleagues and friends but no one shared my apprehension. I concentrated on my dissertation, which I wanted to submit at the earliest possible date; I thought I had found the key to the

---

*The word *ḥay*, celebrating life, is here an acronym formed by inverting the numerals of his father's death date.

understanding of the Tannaites' attitude to Jewish history and to history in general. My hope was that this thesis and the doctoral degree will help me to find an academic position – somewhere.

The Nazis shouted more than the Communists, and it looked as if they would be dominant in the forthcoming election to the Reichstag.

One evening Anne and I were returning home from a party; a friend offered to bring us home in his car. Suddenly we found ourselves surrounded by yelling, screaming, threatening masses who were having (or had) a political demonstration. Many Nazi flags were in evidence; the faces around us were aflame with zeal and passionate hate. Our friend tried his best to figure out how to get to a side street and out of the riotous crowd. Finally we made it and started to breathe freely. I do not remember whether or not I mentioned it to Anne, but that evening I decided to leave Germany, come what may.

The strange thing was that, despite the tension and uncertainty of not knowing what the next day will bring, Anne and I planned to have a baby; Anne conceived at the end of February or beginning of March, 1933. Was it the affirmation of life in the face of the threatening hardship?

Actually we did not have to worry so much; Anne's parents had in ample time moved to London, where her father for several years maintained a branch of his business, and we could always find a temporary shelter. But we were concerned not with the ultimate but the immediate steps to be taken.

On March 30, we tidied up our recently furnished apartment, paid in advance rent to our landlord (a Nazi, though a "friendly" one), packed two or three suitcases, locked the front door and made our way to the station, as unobtrusively as possible, trying to look innocent, unharried. We bought tickets to Paris; our passports were valid still. The train was half empty. We were apprehensive (a possible examination of reason for leaving the country) until the train reached the French border. The French officer who came in to check passports and luggage was looked upon as a friend.

We stayed a few days in Paris, on the Left Bank. Normally, the coffee shops would have provided a special pleasure and a feeling of youthful freedom from care. Now, however, it was especially Anne who was burdened by new pregnancy and the nervous notion of carrying the child –

where to? Palestine was indeed on our mind, so there was no panic. To let the child be born in Germany was out of the question. I myself might have been of some use in Germany as a teacher in the Jewish community, which expected to be more and more excluded from the normal civic life and institutions.

The papers brought the news that as of April 1, a number of Jewish members of university faculties have been given temporary leaves of absence from their duties (*zur Zeit beurlaubt*) — and I among them. This was not unexpected and I took it to be a first step toward more radical procedures against Jews and persons of Jewish ancestry.

We continued our journey to London; Anne's parents stayed at a hotel and we took a room in a less expensive hotel (Strand Palace). Members of the Stiebel-Fränkel families used to assemble in the Stiebel hotel room to discuss plans for the immediate future. Anne's father was expected to know all the answers and, very importantly, to supply funds for relocation and/or resettlement. These meetings and the endless discussions of possibilities or the lack of them exhausted Anne and myself and we were always glad to breathe fresh air outside.

In the meantime we got to know Herbert Loewe, reader in rabbinics at Cambridge University and lecturer in Hebrew at University College in London. The Loewes (his father was secretary to Sir Moses Montefiore and his travelling companion) befriended us generously and, after several meetings, offered me the lectureship at University College (the Goldsmith lectureship) and made the necessary application to the authorities. Privately he was assured that the appointment would indeed materialize. I accepted tentatively, for I wanted to explore my chances in Jerusalem. Anne's father secured an introduction to Judah L. Magnes, president of the Hebrew University.

Loewe invited me to a high tea at his College at Cambridge. The problem of the day was, naturally, the situation in Germany. I voiced my view that the change in the political climate does not make the impression of something transitory. The dons — especially the historians among them, who were interested in meeting a recently dismissed (or furloughed) colleague from Germany — thought that Hitler cannot possibly last in a highly developed and highly literate country such as Germany. I knew that historians are not prophets, but thought they possessed a historical sense to know that there are factors in history other than economic or organizational ones.

I don't know how I happened to be invited to meet the Chief Rabbi, Dr. Joseph Hertz, but here I was, hoping to hear from him a word of wisdom. After showing me various memorabilia, prominently displayed in a glass cabinet, and explaining their significance, the conversation turned to Germany and its Jewry. Hertz, convinced of his importance (after all, he ruled over the Jewish faithful and not so faithful in the entire Commonwealth), advised me that Hitler must fall; as far as I was concerned, I would be able to return "home" in a matter of three months or so.

I doubted it and explained my impression. Finally he asked: "So, how long, you think, will he last?" I answered: "Ten years!" He brushed this aside, as something utterly impossible. Before Hertz asked the question, I did not think in terms of years. But when he asked I was forced to answer and from the subconscious it popped out: Ten years. Well, the terrible period lasted twelve years, rather close to my "prediction." I wished I were wrong and the ecclesiastic right.

We celebrated the Passover Seders with the Stiebels and some members of the family at Mrs. Friedlaender's guest house. The old-fashioned dining room was crowded. Anne's father conducted the Seder, then came the meal. Mrs. Friedlaender brought in a rather large fish upon which she put a gold coin, for good luck. She pronounced some prayer that sounded like a magic formula. No one was exceedingly happy over the exodus from Egypt, having in mind the exodus in which we were personally involved.

Our decision was to go to Palestine. First we went to greet my mother in Tel Aviv, my brother Bernhard and my sisters Fanny and Dvorah. Little Dvorah, deeply involved in a youth movement, was so convinced that Eretz Yisrael is the land of young settlers and workers that she simply asked us: "Are you not much too old to attempt to find a place here for yourselves?" With thirty years behind me, I indeed felt to be a mature man (Anne was just 23 then and expecting a baby) — but not too old to make a second start in life. The land looked young and fresh and everything breathed promise. Dr. Magnes had nothing for me ("Stick around, perhaps a job may develop"), but Dr. Arthur Biram, director of the renowned Reali in Haifa, offered me half a position, starting in September. First I hesitated, for having taught at a University, I felt it wrong to accept a position at a lower institution. What finally persuaded us to accept was the fact that S. D.

Goitein and Ernst Simon had taught at the Reali and that at present Ye-hezkel Kaufman, Joshua Guttman, and Martin Plessner would serve at the Reali with me. And: this job is better than no job and soon they will call me to the Hebrew University. (At the time I knew nothing of the cumber-some appointment procedure at the Hebrew University.) We settled down and took a nice apartment in the newly built house, Balfour Street 13, in walking distance to the Reali. In the meantime came the official appoint-ment to the Goldsmith-lectureship in London; it was personally unpleas-ant to reject it and to explain the complicated situation to Herbert Loewe. I think he never forgave me.

Haifa 1934–1937

After one year at Biram's school and no job in sight at the Hebrew Univer-sity, we knew that we should have to leave the country. I tried to regain the lectureship in London, but the position was now in other hands. I regret-ted that I was so eager to reject the offer when it was made. Now I waited for a new opportunity. I took English lessons (from Shulamith Kastein, who as Greta Vogel, had come from Vienna to marry Joseph Kastein).

I selected and translated midrashic sayings for the *Jüdische Rundschau* and articles on biblical topics (*Das Schriftwort*), did an anthology for the Maimonides year 1935* (Rabbi Mosche ben Maimon) and, commissioned by the Schocken Verlag, worked on a history of the Talmudic Era (*Ge-schichte der talmudischen Zeit*) which appeared in 1937.

The Reali became a full time job and required much time and energy. A small group of students met once a week in our home to discuss prob-lems of the day; I observed with apprehension the fierce nationalism of the young boys and girls. The school asked me to work out the pamphlet on the Bible and its history and collaborate with a colleague on a book— *Aggadah la-Yeladim* (Aggada for children), based on Bialik's *Sefer ha-Ag-gadah*. Upon Biram's suggestion the Vaad Leumi appointed me a member of its Educational Committee, which meant trips to Jerusalem to attend the meetings. David Yellin and Benzion Dinaburg (Dinur) were members of the group.

I translated several stories by S. Y. Agnon into German for the *Jüdische Rundschau* and for a volume of Agnon stories (*In der Gemeinschaft der*

*Commemorating the 600th anniversary of Maimonides' death

Frommen), to which Gershom Scholem contributed translations of three stories.[9] In addition I translated *Ha-Niddah* (*Der Verstossene*).[10]

The Agnon translations brought me in a closer contact with the author, who attached considerable importance to the rendition of his works into other languages, especially into German. He took the time to point to allusions, hidden meanings, hinted references and other subtleties, and I was happy to have the chance to converse with this thoroughly intriguing writer.

I gave a lecture course in the Agudah le-Hishtalmut ba-Madda (People's University) in Haifa and a lecture to a large audience one Saturday afternoon (Technion). On the way home up the Hadar ha-Carmel, I chanced to walk next to a man who criticized the lecture without noticing that I walked next to him. The talk was on Yohanan ben Zakkai and the critic felt there was nothing new in the lecture and the delivery was bad. This gave me a shock and I made the decision to change my style. (Success was slow in coming.)

So I was very busy. Physically, I felt bad — headaches, dizziness, jaundice — probably all psychosomatic discomfort. The best help came from Nahum Sternberg.[11] The summers were very hot and long.

In the last period (1936–37), I did service at the roof of Telsch Hotel observing the neighboring Arab villages; my co-guardian was Shlomo Bardin, head of a nautical school in Haifa, who lived in our neighborhood. Our job was to inform a central office by phone in case of some suspicious movement. Nothing happened. Most unpleasant were the walks home; there were bushes on both sides of the street and a sniper could have easily attacked us without being detected. The political situation in the country became increasingly precarious; the Arabs violently displayed their nationalism and the anti-Zionist stance.

It became clear that the best for us would be to leave the country. I hated to realize that and to admit it to myself. I pretended — both to myself and to others — that we were taking a year's leave and would surely return.

My scholarly plans were set: I wanted to continue my *Tannaiten** into a study of the historical conception of the Amoraim, and an extensive study of the Talmudic-midrashic attitude to biblical prophets and prophecy. Especially the latter occupied by mind completely.

*Glatzer's dissertation, entitled *Untersuchungen zur Geschichtslehre der Tannaiten*[12]

Daniel

Our son was born December 3, 1933, at a private hospital in Haifa. Anne's room was dingy, the corridors loud, the doctor (and owner of the hospital) unreliable, the nurses unfriendly and inefficient; for years Anne remembered this experience. In the evening I was sent away; I went home and, in order to take my nervous mind off the big event, read a learned article on some aspect of Aramaic grammar. Finally I fell asleep; in the morning I phoned the hospital. "He yoledet ben" (she is giving birth to a boy), the nurse told me. I got frantic, for if she already knew it is a boy, how could she "be giving" birth; therefore something must be wrong.*"Please speak German," I pleaded with the nurse, who had tried to practice her beginner's Hebrew on me. Well, nothing but the grammar was wrong. I rushed to the hospital; Anne was exhausted; the boy was brought in and opened his mouth in a mighty yawn. I left, to arrive at school in time for the first class. The school's discipline required that one does one's duty like a soldier. In the recess I informed Biram of the event, using the first words of Isaiah 9:5: "A child is born unto us, a son was given unto us." Biram, with the voice of a prophet: "He will be a teacher in Israel"— the highest achievement he could think of at the moment.

I telephoned my mother, congratulated her and asked her to bring a lot of cookies for the feast of Circumcision. The circumcisor was to be Dr. Joseph Prager, originally from Cassel, a friend of Rosenzweig, who in 1922 had performed the rite on Rosenzweig's son, Rafael.

We had decided long ago to name our child, should it be a boy, Daniel, to commemorate my father's name. In the "secular" version of the name we added Franz, in memory of Franz Rosenzweig. Later on, it was important to our boy that he bears the name of his grandfather, as I inherited my grandfather's name.

Anne required some more time to recover; they had treated her badly, medically and personally. We engaged Alice (later Milwidsky), Anne's cousin, a nurse, to come and look after mother and child.

Daniel was a very handsome little boy. He loved his toys, but was especially eager to listen to classical music on records, Beethoven, Brahms, Mozart. His Hebrew was somehow slow in coming, since there was so

*The phrase, an archaizing expression (cf. Genesis 17:19; Isaiah 7:15), is in the present tense.

much German spoken around the house. But in Kindergarten he did learn Hebrew songs, dances, and stories. On Sabbath mornings, we used to go to the Elijah cave that served as a synagogue. (That was after we moved to Mt. Carmel, Beth Heuser). He liked especially the song *ve-taher libenu* ("O purify our heart to serve thee in truth").

He looked forward to the Sabbath festivities: *nelekh le-bet ha-kneset, nashir ve-taher libenu* ... (We'll go to synagogue, we'll sing "O purify our heart ..."). His friend was Emanuel (Klemperer) whom he called *mamale*. I taught him to recite the biblical first day of creation in Hebrew. In the Kindergarten the children learned *artzah alinu* ("We ascended to our land"), *salenu al ktefenu* ("Our basket upon our shoulders"), *anu banu artzah* ("We came up to our land"), *tu bi-shvat higia* ("The fifteenth day in [the month] Shevat has come") for the New Year of the Trees that was observed by the dressed-up children planting little trees.

But the little boy never looked really happy. He was in no way disturbed, just very quiet, at times moody and a bad sleeper. Among ourselves Anne and I had the notion that this behavior had to do with Anne's pregnancy in an anxious period in our life. One summer we planned a short vacation and brought him to a children's home on Mt. Carmel. He did not want to let us go, though we told him we would soon come back and take him home. When we finally left — I had to tear myself away — he looked after us, sadly, longingly. Later we regretted this scene, thinking that this parting may have had a traumatic impact on him and evoked some feeling of alienation, abandonment. Of course we came soon back from our vacation, which was no vacation.

On the way from the Kindergarten home (I used to fetch him) we passed by a big hole in the ground. We recited *ve-ha-bor rek en bo mayim* ("the ditch was empty, there was no water in it")* from the Joseph story. When he was sick, he expected the doctor to heal him (*ha-dod yetaken et ze*, the uncle will repair it). A general feeling of discomfort he described: *ve-ve beten, ve-ve regel, ve-ve yad, ve-ve rosh* (woe the stomach, woe the foot, woe the hand, woe the head). He wanted to catch the bird from the window sill* (*tzipor ba yad*, the bird [should be] in [my] hand). He liked new clothes (*lilbosh hadash*, to put on [something] new). He exclaimed: *o zeh tov* (oh, that is good). He identified the phrase with honey; he requested *lehem im o zeh tov* (bread with "oh that is good"). He was proud of his tall figure:

*Genesis 37:24

64

Daniel gadol mipo-mipo-mipo-mipo (Daniel is big from here to here to here). On finding his parents lying in bed in the morning, he declared: *day abba lishon* [he said *isson*] *imma,* which must have meant: Enough for daddy to sleep with mummy, and: let me now sleep with mummy. When Franz Meyer visited, we introduced him as "Uncle Franz." He understood "Uncle Brahms" and was all in awe to meet the great composer in person. We had to correct him and in correcting disappoint him.

Josie's Bat Mitzvah

We had been attending Friday evening services at the Berlin chapel at Brandeis University. Much singing, good participation of students, male and female, an element of Hasidism and the personal involvement of Rabbi Al Axelrad – all this was accepted with pleasure, especially by Josie.[13] We decided to celebrate her Bat Mitzvah there, shortly before her twelfth birthday. The Torah reading was the concluding portion of Leviticus, which includes the famous words: "On the Jubilee year proclaim liberty throughout the land and all its inhabitants." The prophetic portion was Jeremiah 16:19 to 17:14, starting "O Lord, my strength and my stronghold, my refuge in the time of trouble," and ending, "Heal me, O Lord, and I shall be healed; save me and I shall be saved; for thou art my praise." She used to come to study and we rehearsed the benedictions on the Torah and the prophetic portion, the chant of the haftarah and the responses during the service, especially the chants of taking out the Torah from the Ark and the returning of the Scroll.

Josie was beautifully tall, her hair parted and partly covered. She read and sang with beautiful fluency and conviction. When she finished, she was pelted, according to custom, with raisins and nuts; she smiled. Then she and I ascended the pulpit next to the Torah shrine; she gave her speech first, a text she wrote herself, without my "help." She spoke of my attitude to Judaism which is, she said, based on prayer, tradition, ritual; hers is an attitude to community; she feels she belongs to the community of Israel, a community such as symbolized by this very group. I spoke of what history and the past means to a few; how the past lives on in the present. I referred to "Proclaim liberty . . ." of today's Torah portion, a phrase that was inscribed on the Liberty Bell in Philadelphia; the bell cracked and is out of commission; the word has not cracked; it lives on. At the end I blessed her, using the feminine form of the verbs. The rabbi had the family stand and recite together *shehaheyanu*,* in gratitude that we were privileged to live this day.

Josie was in a happy mood throughout. I hope she will remember the event later in life and will keep alive the importance of the prayer book and the Bible and that she will establish a good Jewish home.

Prague, 1970

[Anne and I] decided to make this trip [from Zurich] to commemorate 1920 when I left Bohemia. We were booked in a four (or five) star hotel, but it was a run-down place and less than comfortable. We decided not to speak to each other (except technicalities) for the room might be bugged. Among the guests were many Arabs, probably businessmen, who felt very much at home there. The table with newspapers displayed only Czech, Russian, and Arabic journals. Anne was apprehensive. The food was abominable; *versputenka* (entertainment) was part of the bill; the piano player concentrated on a song "California"— I guess that is where he wanted to be.

We took a streetcar to downtown; the cars may have been the very same I knew in 1920; the conductors were women, badly dressed in their formless uniforms; people shabbily attired, both men and women. The mood was rather oppressive, or rather depressed. No coffeehouses, the churches closed.

Schocken asked me to contact in Prague a writer who could represent Kafka's Prague on a *gremium* [council] that was being formed for the historical-critical edition of Kafka's works. I phoned to the Czech writers' guild and was given an evasive answer. I tried to phone the writer but there were too many people by that name in the phone book. After several attempts I gave up.

We went to the Alt-Neu Shul which is now a museum, as is the old cemetery and the other synagogues. The Alt-Neu Shul was packed with tourists, especially from the third-world countries. A guide did some explaining. A man pointed to my French cap, meaning I should take it off in this holy place. I misunderstood him and thought he did not notice my head cover (the synagogue is rather dim) and wanted me to cover my head. Then I no-

*Prayer expressing gratitude for being sustained in life to reach a special occasion

66

ticed that he had no head cover and the situation became quite clear. He did not know that this was a Jewish place of worship and that Jews cover their heads.

Behind the Alt-Neu Shul is the ancient cemetery. The old tombstones stand in odd shapes one next to the other, the lettering barely legible. They point accusingly toward heaven. Most tourists go to the tomb of the Maharal (Rabbi Loewe ben Bezalel), the creator of the legendary Golem in Prague. I guess the guide spoke of the rabbi as a worker of miracles. Other great men, scholars and saints, are buried here. In the Nazi period, children were allowed to use the cemetery as their only playground (before the edict of destruction was issued).

The Maisel synagogue guards a large collection of *parahot*, curtains before Torah shrines. Most of them are most beautifully embroidered, the colors exquisite, the lettering well proportioned.

I inquired about the origin of this remarkable collection. The Nazis, in destroying the countless small Jewish communities in Bohemia and Moravia, took away the curtains to be deposited in one place and become accessible to "research." When the Nazi regime collapsed, the collection came into the possession of the Russians. The curtains are expertly displayed, catalogued; naturally, the place of origin is duly noted. What is not noted is that once upon a time (not long ago, but still in one's lifetime), there were Jewish communities and honest prayer, and when the curtain was moved aside and the shrine of the Torah opened, the worshipers rose in honor of the Torah and exclaimed, "Blessed be he who gave the Torah to his people Israel in his holiness."

A short distance from the Alt-Neu Shul we noticed a "synagoga restaurant." We assumed that should be a kosher eating place. We came closer; the menu did not sound kosher or Jewish. Inside were regular townspeople, smoking, drinking beer and talking loud. The place bore its name simply because it was near the *synagoga*; nothing more was implied.

I reflected on the fact that where Jews live, a term such as *synagogue* can only be used with reference to Jews. Only when they are gone — died out, expelled or destroyed — terms once meaningful can (and will) become neutral designations.

I wanted to see Bodenbach again, the town I left in 1920, leaving parents, brother and sister behind for a while. A bus line leads from Prague to Dečin (formerly Tetschen, which incorporates Bodenbach, the Czech

Podmokly). Pleasant view of the landscape; fields, meadows, here and there a farm. Statues of saints along the road; their heads chopped off – I guess, in an anti-Church campaign. Finally – the city square of Děčin.

Not too much change, only that Czech has replaced the German language. We made our way to my Gymnasium; now there is a Czech inscription on the gate. I approach the gate; it was closed; through the glass window I could see the flight of stairs. I trembled in remembering my fears and dread of 1916 to 1920. Back we went and over the bridge to Bodenbach via main street to the corner where you ascend to the Schäferwand. To the right is the Temple. The lower entrance, which used to lead to the Cantor's apartment, was closed. The Temple, too, was closed. I rang the bell and a caretaker opened the door. I could not enter, he said; that is now a state archive; there is only one room on the first floor, reserved for the Jewish community. He wanted to give me the address of the community's leader but I declined. I stood long, contemplating and remembering my early years. On to Schäferwand-Strasse 7, where we used to live during the war and shortly after. The house stands but changed name and number. A gate, closed, guards the entrance to the apartments. The terrace adjoining the house is still there but completely overgrown with bushes. The ascent was steeper than I remembered it.

I enjoyed showing Anne the sights, the streets, squares, buildings, especially the house we lived in and the Temple. By the way, the Temple is much smaller than I remembered it. The shack where the "Alter Melammed" lived is no more; the waterfront at this part of the Elbe was changed.

We were hungry but saw no attractive (or even just acceptable) place. Finally we spotted a possible eating place. The trouble was that the menu was all in Czech with no hint of German or French; neither the waiter nor the owner knew any German. Finally a customer came to try to help us, but was unable to explain anything. Anne did not feel well; the heat was intense and oppressive. We hurried to the railway station and found a train leading back to Prague. In the compartment sat a woman; the tattooed number on her arm marked her as a former prisoner in a Concentration Camp. She asked for advice how she could possibly come to the United States. We promised to write her the address of an organization to help survivors. She said how happy she was to have met us; it might have changed her life.

Mona Lisa

When the "Mona Lisa" was stolen from the Louvre in Paris in 1911 and was missing for two years, more people went to stare at the blank space than had gone to look at the masterpiece in the twelve previous years.

How true that is. Long ago Prague hosted a thriving Jewish community, with its pious men and women, its saints, its children; little synagogues where worshipers assembled twice a day to offer hymns to the Lord of All; orphanages, hospitals, and lodgings for the wayfarer. The surrounding Gentile city knew: here live the Jews. They think they are as good as we are, say the Gentiles, but we know that this is not so. Let us avoid them and their habitations. Some say that the Golem, that dead monster, lies up there, in the Synagogue's attic.

All that has changed since the Evil One did his frightful work in Europe's cities, towns, villages. Nothing is left of the former glory and splendor, nothing but one ancient Synagogue and an even more ancient cemetery.

But now the "world" no longer avoids the site. Now they come from all over Europe to visit the former Jewish Ghetto. They buy tickets to enter the Jewish museum — for all the remnants of Jewish life have become a museum and property of the State. They come to visit the ancient Synagogue and reverently listen to the explanations of the guide; they visit the ancient cemetery and especially the grave site of the creator of the Golem, Rabbi Loewe ben Bezalel. They visit the hall where hundreds of Torah curtains are carefully displayed (once upon a time they adorned the Torah arks of synagogues that were scattered throughout the land).

There is much to be seen in that Museum. But life has departed. Many men, women and children died in Concentration Camps and the life of the rest has come to an end.

The picture is gone. What is left of the rest is the memory of what the frame contained. People come from all over to admire the empty frame and the narrow space enclosed by the frame. Does this mean that the frame is more attractive, better still, more meaningful than the precious pictures? Or, perhaps, the meaning is that people, in admiring the frame, demonstrate their inability to regard the picture? Or, perhaps, it is that people do not admire the frame, but the cruel act that removed the picture and left the empty space behind. The admiration thus would be accorded to cruelty, vandalism, and destructiveness.

Going to a Kafka Meeting

A meeting of the editors of the projected critical edition of Kafka's works was called for July 11, 1973 to take place in Herzog August Bibliothek, Wolfenbuttel, of which Paul Raabe was director.

Since I was in Oxford at the time and Malcolm Pasley, the Kafka scholar, is an Oxonian, we arranged to go together. He fetched me the previous day, July 10, by car and we drove to London. We arrived in time to take the 9:40 plane for Hanover, which we reached at 11:00. No problem getting a bus from the air terminal to the railway station, where we conveniently made a train to Braunschweig. An easy, short ride. Raabe's secretary named the hotel we were to stay overnight. Some kind of electrical train was ready to take us to Wolfenbuttel. Everything was so simple and smooth, and we congratulated ourselves for being a perfect team. A brief taxi ride brought us to a little hotel.

Now the unexpected happened: the gate was locked and a slip of paper informed us that "I (the hotel keeper) will return at 3:15." A minor nuisance but the Kafka symbolism was striking. When everything goes well you expect no further obstacle and there it comes: the locked gate of a lodging at mid-day. I must assume that Kafka appeared to the hotel keeper in a dream and asked him to close the gate on that day and hour. Otherwise we would be ill-prepared for an editorial conference on Kafka. There will never be an undisturbed, quietly fulfilled, unworried Kafka.

Jerusalem

I was invited by the convener of a Franz Rosenzweig symposium (Paul Mendes-Flohr, a former student of mine) to participate; Anne and I were glad to be able to make this trip. Flohr and Yehuda Reinharz fetched us from the Lod airport and brought me to Bet Belgia; Richard [Stiebel] came to call for us.[14] The symposium was well prepared, the participants well versed in Rosenzweig's writings. Rafael Rosenzweig attended but stressed that he had no real interest in the proceedings. Of old-timers there was Scholem, who opened the congress, and Ernst Simon, who reminisced about the period. My paper was on the concept of language in Rosenzweig's thought; also, I responded to André Neher's paper on "Rosenzweig and Kafka" and chaired the presentation of a videotaped interview with

Edith Rosenzweig.[15] I took this occasion to confess that, at the time, I underestimated the contribution of Edith R. He, Rosenzweig, was to me all important and I took Edith R. for granted. Later on I realized my misjudgment and would have liked to ask her forgiveness. As things are in life, I never did; all I have now is a feeling of deep regret.

Judy had mentioned before we left Boston that she may show up in Jerusalem. She sent a cable from Paris and came; Anne fetched her from the airport. We stayed at Mishkenot Sha'ananim as guests of the city of Jerusalem. The most beautiful, captivating, inspiring thing was the view from the balcony. You faced a part of the wall of Jerusalem and some old establishments. To the right you saw *Ge-Hinnom*, the Valley of Hinnom, Gehenna, Hell. In the distance villages and modern developments, to the right a Scottish monastery (that in the war of 1948 supplied food to Israel defense forces fighting to retain Jerusalem). The Mishkenot was defended by a single Jewish soldier; he fell and is memorialized by a tablet on the premises and in the adjoining Sephardic synagogue.

Judy and I stood there on the balcony, mostly silent, in admiration of the *genius loci*. We thought of ancient Jerusalem, people who lived here, and the meaning of Jerusalem in Jewish life through the ages. Then Judy spoke: She loved this place when she spent a year at Hebrew University. Then the strong impression weakened and she started to doubt Jerusalem's significance to her. She felt she had come here to "find out." She found, she said, that only here she has a deep feeling of belonging. This is a force that cannot be argued about, or its existence proven. I was happy to hear that and added that my attitude is similar to hers. This is not a nationalist feeling; there is room for everybody here. Silence again, awe, and gratitude. We were both drawn to this majestic view. School children came by, singing, on to visit the wall and to continue to Mt. Zion. Young strong voices. That added to the picture as a whole.

Midrash

Before we left Germany in 1933, there was a little party at the Martin Plessners. The talk turned toward the political conditions in the country. Nobody realized the seriousness of the situation; still a feeling of uncertainty prevailed. What do we do if worse comes to worse? The clever Eugen Mayer (then the administrator of the Frankfurt Jewish community) pointed to me: "Glatzer has nothing, to worry; he takes his little Tanakh [Bible] and will always find a place for himself. Besides, *Glatzer hat die Manteltaschen/Voll verwandelter Midrashen,** and that should help."

Indeed, I had already published a variety of *midrashim* in German translation; *Sendung und Schicksal* contained some selections, and *Gespräche der Weisen*, prepared long before its publication, was based on midrashic materials. So were the *Merksprüche* from Talmud and Midrash that Robert Weltsch published in *Jüdische Rundschau* in 1935 and 1937.[16] In the forties in this country I contemplated a comprehensive collection of midrashic teachings in English. Salman Schocken persuaded me to produce a concise selection to fit the size of the Schocken Library volumes, i.e., 128 pages. (I agreed, in the hope that an opportunity would arise for a more substantial volume). The intention was to help the reader discover the profundity of thought, the depth of faith, and the beauty of form that the Midrash offers. But the full project was never realized and nobody else did the work;[17] Montefiore and Loewe's *Rabbinic Anthology* is fine, but too well organized; the midrashic form is disregarded, and there are too many discussions (though some interesting ones) between the two editors.

Before publication, Salman Schocken invited some of the editorial staff of *Commentary* to discuss the publication, promotion, and my treatment of classical Hebrew material. Of the animated prolonged discussion I remember only one thing: One of the big editors thought it was a pity that the phrase "Said Rabbi so and so" occurs over and over again and that scriptural verses were quoted in practically every selection. If this kind of reference were omitted, this volume could become a best seller, or at least a book of general interest, comparable to selections of Chinese wisdom or Buddhist teachings.

He felt that an expression of pure faith or of human insight must lose its value if presented as the meaning of a biblical sentence or the essence of rabbinic learning. I understood what he meant. He was right – from his point of view. In my way of thinking a midrash must preserve its identity and may not pretend to be a Buddhist saying.

My scholarly plans were to a large degree based on Talmudic-midrashic materials. My Ph.D. dissertation was a presentation of the concept of history developed and maintained by the Tannaites (*Untersuchungen zur Geschichtslehre der Tannaiten: Ein Beitrag zur Religiongeschichte* [1932].[18] I

*Glatzer has his coatpocket full of metamorphosed Midrash

collected material for a continuation of this line into the Amoraic period, which work would have served as a *Habilitationschrift* (a thesis towards becoming a *Privatdozent* at the Frankfurt University). Emigration and the uncertainty of the times were in the way; I had to give my time to popular publication.

I did manage to write a little book *Hillel the Elder: The Emergence of Classical Judaism* [1956];[19] there were two revised editions and editions in German and in Spanish. The book was originally commissioned by the B'nai B'rith Hillel Foundation and issued as a paperback by Schocken Books. After three editions I requested that Schocken stop a republication; there were too many passages I would have had to rewrite completely. Yohanan of Tiberias fascinated me and I collected aggadic material on this great Amora of the third century. I used the material in a few scholarly essays but never managed to write a definitive Yohanan.

A serious plan was the writing of a comprehensive presentation of the post-biblical attitude of the Jewish Sages to the phenomenon of prophecy and to the biblical Prophets. I did a monograph-length piece on the topic with copious footnotes (in English). The *Review of Religion* (now defunct) agreed to publish an abridged version; it appeared in 1946;[20] I was happy with this publication. A Hebrew version *Torat ha-Nevuah ba-Talmud*, appeared in *Sefer ha-Shanah le-Yehude Amerika* 1942.[21] The piece is often quoted.

Hannah Arendt invited me to contribute to a projected Festschrift for Adolf Leschnitzer. I worked out an essay on "The Concept of Peace in Classical Judaism," using some of my Yohanan material. My thesis was that the third-century masters and especially Yohanan and his school gave up the claim of the legitimate rule of Jerusalem; now the rule of Rome was recognized as divinely ordained. Judaism withdrew from the realm of history and concentrates on a life with God as the only right existence. The Festschrift appeared in 1961.[22] I wrote "The Concept of Sacrifice in post-Biblical Judaism" when invited to read a paper at the annual conference of the American Society for the Study of Religion.

The paper shows how, with the cessation of sacrifice in the Temple, the concept of *korban** was retained and expanded to be applied to study, prayer, hospitality. In the end most religious and ethical functions were included in the compass of *korban*. It is, however, necessary to consider the

---

*Sacrificial offering

73

original meaning of the term: it points to the nearness of God, man's wish to become near to God. Also terms like that of priest and the altar were similarly interpreted. The essay appeared in my collected Jewish essays, 1978;[23] it requires expansion and a fuller documentation.

Looking back on my scholarly and writing life (1980), I wish I could have given all my energy to the exploration of the Midrash and, in good time, was able to come up with a comprehensive presentation something like "Major Concepts of the Midrashic Masters."

Still, I do not regret that circumstance led me to various projects of a different kind: Rosenzweig's life and thought,[24] the Leopold Zunz letters,[25] the Buber volumes (and now his correspondence),[26] and the Kafka work.[27]

II
Encounters

H. N. Bialik: Hebrew Poet

I read his poetry during World War I and knew some of his songs. In the
early twenties, when Bialik (and other Hebrew writers in the company of
Shoshanah Persitz) resided in Bad Homburg, Agnon encouraged me to pay
a visit to the great poet. I came (after getting an appointment with the
man) and was struck by his urbaneness and simplicity. He inquired what I
was doing and, unexpectedly, asked: "Is eyer Foter ferneglakh?" ("Is your
father well-to-do?") I do not remember my answer. I recall his praise of
the Hebrew language. I was proud to have made the acquaintance of the
poet and returned happily to Frankfurt.

On one of my visits to Israel's Land (in 1927 or 1929) I was asked by Salman Schocken to explain to Bialik why he, Schocken, could not let him use
his Solomon ibn Gabirol material (it was most probably a manuscript that
Schocken wanted to be worked on by his own Institute of Medieval Hebrew Poetry). Bialik showed his dissatisfaction, even anger, for he counted
on Mr. Schocken's courtesy. I had to explain that I acted as messenger only
and had no say in the matter. My "mission" accomplished, I got up to leave.
Bialik said he wanted to walk with me a few steps. Children were playing
in the street and Bialik stood to watch them talking Hebrew. He voiced
his astonishment how natural the children's Hebrew sounded, how Hebrew became the people's normal language. He knew, of course, that he
had a decisive part in this process. Again and again he found groups of
children playing in Hebrew, talking at the top of their voices, and the poet
observed them and the chatter in the language of the Bible.

Saturday afternoons an *oneg Shabbat** took place in Tel Aviv's Bet Am.
The high point of this celebration of the holy day was Bialik's address that
combined prose with poetry, high ideals of Judaism with present national
politics, glory of the past with a vision for the future. On one such occa-

---

*a festive celebration on the Sabbath

sion, Bialik called out: "I predict that one day Tel Aviv will reach the river Yarkon." That sounded like a far-fetched prognosis; the audience readily forgave Bialik such boldness. However, it did not take long and the Yarkon was engulfed by the mightily growing city of Tel Aviv. The visionary's vision was more realistic than the administrator's calculations.

In the early thirties Bialik happened to give one of his public lectures, this time in Haifa. I remember that he criticized those whose Judaism extends "from the pants upward," i.e., the idealists and spiritualizers, while Judaism should include all that is "from the pants downward," i.e., the practical, material, earthly, non-spiritual, non-intellectual in life. The message was not new; we Zionists were used to the call to the soil, to simple, earthly life and thought. But it was a special pleasure to hear all this in Bialik's language, a robust, urbane, at times whimsical, always rich Hebrew.

When the Jewish Theological Seminary was to confer upon Bialik an honorary doctor's degree [1926], he appeared all dressed up in the usual academic cap and gown. Mrs. Bialik, not accustomed to this kind of ceremony, was greatly impressed and looked in awe on her husband. Bialik noticed it and turned to her: "Do not look on me with such admiration; to you I am still the old Hayim Nahman."

I saw him last in 1934, shortly before his trip to Vienna, from which he did not return alive. He was sitting in a bank in the space reserved for employees, counting money. It was a lot of money, or that is what it appeared to be. The impression was one of incongruity. The great Hebrew poet, the great expert in classical Hebrew literature — and money? But, after all, he was also the head of a publishing house, and had to buy and sell and be concerned about making a profit. Still, as an experience it seemed paradoxical and I left the bank, disappointed. The next thing was the news of his death.

S. Y. Agnon

I met him in the early twenties, I do not remember at what occasion. At the time he lived in Homburg, but he occasionally came to Frankfurt for visits, and for exploring Hebrew bookstores. The fact that my father hailed from Buczacz or a townlet nearby impressed Agnon; he used to mention it in the course of the years, though he could not recall a family by the name of Glatzer. Nevertheless he considered me a descendant of an unknown Jew of Buczacz.

Among the young Zionists, stories circulated about the great Hebraists in Bad Homburg—Aḥad Ha-am, Bialik, Ravnizky, Agnon, and Mrs. Shoshana Persitz, who apparently supported them all and printed their works.

The best story concerns Agnon's hernia. This condition was kept a great secret for, apparently, in the thinking of a traditional Jew this is something embarrassing (some connection with sexual activity?). The date was set for Agnon to enter the hospital and have surgery performed. Those involved promised complete secrecy. On that very date a fire broke out in Agnon's house. People gathered: "Where is Agnon, where is Agnon?" Then it "came out" where he was and for what purpose. He must have seen in this coincidence a divine punishment, or, at least, a divine hint of something. Perhaps he had no eagerness to engage in theological reflecting; his entire library and a manuscript of his work went up in flames and Agnon must have seen his entire existence shattered.

In the spring term 1922, Agnon, invited by Rosenzweig, read within the Lehrhaus program his *Aggadat ha-Sofer* ("The Legend of the Scribe"). The reading took place in Rosenzweig's study before about twenty listeners. The voice and the tenor of the reading is still in my ears: it was reverent, humble, submissive, but not tragic. That is how it was ordained to happen and so it happened. The reading convinced me that that was Agnon's interpretation of the story and not as the modern analysts and critics understand it. By the way, after the reading people were encouraged to ask questions, in Hebrew of course. Rosenzweig wrote in a letter that everybody appeared to be able to speak Hebrew but no one did.

Later, in Eretz Israel, I arrived at his house at the time he set for me (I was working on a translation of one of his stories) and heard him studying in a loud, pious voice. I waited before ringing the bell in order to hear as much as possible. Finally a break came and I entered.

The last time I visited him was in 1968, with Anne. Before we came I begged her not to show off her Hebrew but to talk German. His wife was there but no longer communicating. He complained that Schocken does not publish more works of his in English. Tell him "Ani ish mar," (I am a bitter man). Then about his style: "I write simply, things as they are." What an understatement. How are things, anyway! He complained that he did not see me in New York when he visited after receiving the Nobel Prize in 1965; that I was in California at the time was not enough of an excuse. I told him I was preparing an edition of his short stories and showed him a list with

77

the tentative selection. He said he would go over it and return it. I gave him the list but never saw it again. The book appeared in the spring of 1970 under the title *Twenty-One Stories*; he died February 17, 1970.

Arnold Band, who visited the Agnon family after the writer's death, told that in addition to the slip of paper, "Bury me beside a simple school teacher," there was one, saying, "Ule-son'ai lo eslah lo ba-zeh ve-lo ba-ba." (My enemies I shall not forgive in this world and not in the next.) Who would be his enemies but the critics who often misread him and prevented an even greater popularity.

Still, he was the only Hebrew writer to receive (part of) the Nobel Prize for Literature. Ted Schocken told me that Agnon could not fall asleep the night before the event. He wanted to press the button to put on the light. He pressed the wrong button and in came "a shikse und sogar eine schöne." And then, at the very special banquet (only for the winners and the royal family), the hosts served him a fish, the kashrut of which was previously established by the local rabbinate; but Agnon insisted meekly that this fish was unknown to him, and only his wife would have been able to render a decision. After a quick conference by the chefs, the question was put to him whether a piece of herring would be acceptable. "Herring — ja." And so it was. A plate with a piece of herring was ushered in, in contrast to all the delicacies and rare foods that the other guests received. A *Yid* is in *Golus*,* even if he gets a Nobel Prize, even in the presence of a King, and possibly, especially in such a situation.

Some Hebrew literature experts opine that the true Agnon is the cynic, the doubter, indeed, almost a non-believer. His piety and religious observance is, they say, but a facade. "The Legend of the Scribe" depicts the tragic life and the sorry end of whoever honestly observes modern Jewish life. *Sofer* means both a Torah scribe and the writer. The house of prayer and study (in "A Guest for the Night") is almost empty and only the prayer for the dead is recited by mourners. The visitor receives the key to the once hallowed house and promptly loses it.

I do not deny that this is a possible interpretation, but I do not believe that it is the correct one. I think Agnon sees the decay and destruction of much of ancient Jewish values and the fragility of Jewish existence. But he himself lives (well, lived) in that world which by now is but a legend, a

*Viz., A Jew is in exile

78

tale. It is a lonely world for few, if any, can be his companions. But it is the only world that he can recognize as real – and which can recognize him. He feels (well, felt) that he is the only authentic Hebrew writer today and that is not a vanity or boastfulness. That in the end he became paralyzed and bereft of speech can be taken symbolically.

In the world today ("the hospital") the inhabitants are sick; he who wants to speak is not allowed to (paralysis of speech); it would make no sense; but a few signals are needed to maintain life and to survive. The only true end is the end of all: death. To be aware of this, as Agnon was, is a mode of worship, a form of piety. The motif of love, which permeates many of his stories and especially in the posthumously published *Shirah* is an attempt to transcend the tragic element in life, including Jewish life.

Nathan Birnbaum

I knew his rebellious outbursts from his "Mattias Acher" period long before I had occasion to meet him – which happened in 1924 when he came to give a series of lectures at the Lehrhaus. It was known that he had gone through the stages from *Freigeist* ("free spirit") to Zionist and then on to Agudas Yisroel, organized anti-Zionist Orthodoxy. His lectures were on "Essence and Significance of Form in Judaism." He said that forms are essential in every religion. In Judaism they are even more so, since they accompany all aspects of life and thought. Forms in Judaism turn the Jewish people into a "Weltanschauungsorganization." This in turn has the purpose of an ever renewed recognition of the one God and the faithful's relation to Him on the one side, and on the other the task of working toward victory of monotheism and what it implies. This kind of dedicated life involves isolation and discipline. The plan for such life must be accepted in toto; all its provisions are of equal importance.

What he was driving at was Orthodoxy, but he gave it an intellectual, civilizational, moralistic underpinning. "Culture" is to be accepted, only *entgottete* (god-less) culture rejected. That is the rub, I thought. "Culture" does not make such distinction.

The *Israelit* published a short review of mine,[28] but added an editorial note to the effect that "the concept of religious purity of traditional Judaism cannot tolerate that from the same podium today radical *kefiroh* (apostasy) is being proclaimed and tomorrow loyalty to Torah and commandments." "Academic freedom is unknown to the Halakhah." This criticism of the Lehrhaus did much to alienate me further from organized Orthodoxy and its religious militancy.

But Birnbaum (who later on became fed up with Agudas Yisroel) was different: he was a man in search and none of his pronouncements sounded final.

After the lectures and the question periods, I usually accompanied him to his hotel. Once he asked me to come up with him and the talk came to Zionism. He told the story of his relationship with Herzl. The latter's vanity repelled Birnbaum (or was it that he did not give due credit to Birnbaum's pre-Herzl Zionist activity?) so that finally he left the Zionist movement. (He mentioned that he coined the term *Zionist*). I was moved by the story of a man who took part in an historical process.

Another time I brought him to the railroad station. He scrutinized the wagons and finally occupied a seat and came out to continue our conversation. Suddenly he asked: "Don't you like to sit opposite a pretty girl?" I don't remember my answer (I cannot possibly have denied it), but I vividly recall my feeling of consternation how an old religious Jew (he was sixty at the time) had pretty girls on his mind, and even more, that he freely admitted it to a young man.

Later, Birnbaum tried to make me join his "Aulim" movement (The Ascending Ones)*and sent me material. I answered politely but refused to join. His *Der Ruf* I received on subscription and had an article published there. I visited him in The Hague (in 1935 or 1936), where he had taken refuge from Hitler. I found an old man, disappointed with official Judaism yet still ready to proclaim a new Judaism of faith, devotion, closeness to nature. He mentioned negotiating with a publisher a translation into German of Bialik's and Ravnitzki's *Sefer ha-Aggadah*. I wondered whether his knowledge of rabbinic Hebrew was sufficiently strong for such a project, but said nothing. He died in 1937.

N. A. Nobel

I heard some members of the Zionist "Blau-Weiss" singing the praises of this rabbi, halakhist, preacher, Goethe enthusiast, mystic. Being a disciple of Solomon Breuer and a student at his yeshivah, it was not easy to have

*I.e., Hebrew *olim*

anything to do with this "antagonist." But something drove me to taste from this forbidden fruit without losing my place in the yeshivah. First I went to the Sabbath services at the Synagoge Borne Platz, especially when Nobel delivered a sermon. These sermons were most unusual. He used to rise to near ecstasy in elucidating a scriptural passage or event. He addressed the silent biblical person, and argued lovingly with him. He gave the most exciting midrashic expositions of his own; the text came alive. The Sabbath and the Festivals were great spiritual events, Judaism a profound spiritual force. Somehow I found myself attending his daily *shiur*, the class in Talmud that took place in a room adjoining both Nobel's residence and the synagogue. I don't remember how I explained my absence to the yeshivah people. Nobel's method in the study of the Talmud was clear-cut, rational, text-oriented, no *pilpul*;* occasionally he referred to "how they say it in the *yeshives*." I appreciated his greater freedom within tradition and the worldly range of the participants. There were private talks with him, and to the still unsettled youngster this contact with the mature man and the prominent Jew was decisive. What the young man needs besides actual instruction is affirmation and some pointing of the way toward a goal. At one of the talks he urged me to drop my Germanic first name in favor of my Hebrew name Nahum. This made much sense to me and I started to be called Nahum; only members of my family continued referring to me as Norbert, and some cousins still do so today. At another meeting, Nobel pressed me to his body, enwrapped me in his coat and blessed me.

I was gripped as by a mystical experience. It seemed I heard the text before; but in Nobel's recitation, it was an unbelievable force. Later, when I studied the Tractate *Berakhot* with care, I detected the blessing. Also, later it occurred to me that Nobel, though married and father of a daughter, may have had homosexual leanings and the whole scene was an erotic event in so far as the rabbi was concerned.

At that study circle was a man who was said to have returned recently from the war and who was a *ba'al teshuvah*, a Jew who found his way from Jewish indifference to total commitment. This was Franz Rosenzweig, who had come to Frankfurt to reorganize the Jüdische Volkshochschule in what was to become the Freies Jüdisches Lehrhaus. Nobel and the

*Casuistry

administrator of the Jewish community of Frankfurt, Dr. Eugen Mayer, were instructed to offer the position to Rosenzweig. The latter, who possibly "knew" less than most of us, impressed us by an incisive way of asking questions and of seeing clearly what the text was driving at. He must have talked to me (as he talked to others) because at a point he invited me to come to his study group at the Lehrhaus on Hermann Cohen's *Religion der Vernunft* that took place at his home, Schumann-Strasse 10. An enduring relationship ensued.

When Nobel's fiftieth birthday (1921) was approaching, Rosenzweig organized a *Feier der Jugend* (youth celebration), to which the entire community was invited. The event took place in the Frankfurt Loge. Ernst Simon gave a glorious tribute, a group played Peretz's *Die goldene Kette* (in which I played the rabbi), an a capella choir sang Mendelssohn's Psalm 100, and Nobel answered. The rehearsals took up much time, which I for one most willingly wasted. The celebration left us with a warm glow and even with a feeling of achievement. Alas, it was one of the last things Nobel could take part in. Soon after the celebration he took ill and the rumor spread that he would not survive. The disciples were asked to keep vigil at his sickbed; the Ḥevra kadishah (Holy Brotherhood)* came to recite Psalms. On the last day he was in a coma. We stood around his bed and joined in the recital of Psalms. Only when he seemed to awaken were we given a sign to stop so that he will not notice and become aware of his situation — possibly an infantile precaution. Time passed and we were told that the rabbi had died.** The Ḥevra kadishah did its job; it moved into the bedroom with the washing utensils and washed the body quickly, first in the lying, then in a standing position. The funeral procession started from his home. A multitude stood in the street. Slowly we followed the bier down the steps. The closing of the hearse made a sharp noise, disturbing the quiet around us. And on to the cemetery, on foot of course. We students arrived early and found the grave ready to receive the body. The guard tried to move us away. One of us called: "Ich bin a Talmid" (I am a student [of his]), and the rather demented guard (or grave digger) answered: "A talmid hin, a talmid her"— which cannot be translated.

Strange, I knew well what happened, but was yet too young to understand the reality of death. A romantic, mystical notion of life prevented this. Understanding came much much later.

*Traditional designation for a Jewish burial society. **In 1922

Martin Buber
The First Meeting

By 1918–19 I had read Buber's *Drei Reden*, *Rabbi Nahman*, the article "Der Mythos der Juden" (in the volume *Vom Judentum*), and was, like many other young Jews, impressed. It was the harmonious combination of Judaic sources and the modern, Western style that appealed to me. When I came to Frankfurt, in 1920, I decided to visit the great man in Heppenheim where he had moved from Berlin in 1916. First, however, I needed my father's permission since it was known that Buber was not an observing Jew. Father was apprehensive but gave his permission, provided I agree not to become influenced by Buber's brand of religiosity. I don't know how he imagined this type of communication to work.

I wrote a letter to Buber, introducing myself, and received an answer by his secretary giving me a date for the meeting.[29] I was thrilled and spent days in preparing myself for the event. I took a train, reached Heppenheim, inquired where Buber lived and found the house with the name plate: Dr. Buber. He opened the door and received me in the dining room. His eyes (wild, deep, intent) inquired, what brings you here? I did not expect this question, but now I did have to say something. Rather bewildered I asked whether his retelling of hasidic stories are not too far removed from the often crude, inelegant originals. In other words (which I did not use): Don't you introduce the aesthetic element and thus distort the literature you wish to present to the public? I immediately noticed that I had criticized his work, while all I wanted was contact, instruction, etc. My blunt remarks pushed him into a defensive position. He explained his method, which in the course of time I learned to appreciate and even to imitate in my attempts to present midrashic materials to the modern reader. I did not stay long for my goal to face the great man was achieved in the first few minutes. When I left, I had the feeling of having undergone an important experience.

Lehrhaus

January to March 1922 Buber gave his lectures in Rosenzweig's Freies Jüdisches Lehrhaus: "Religion als Gegenwart," followed by seminar sessions where he read and explained hasidic texts (i.e. stories). The lectures were held on Sunday in the auditorium of the Hochsche Konservatorium and were a moving experience. The subject matter was drawn from the material that went into *I and Thou*, which appeared in 1923.[30] A smaller group assembled for hasidic stories; through the program stated that "Knowledge of Hebrew is desired," it was not necessary; the texts were taken from *Der grosse Maggid*, which appeared in 1922. Buber explained not only the meaning of a given story but also the midrashic-Talmudic background of certain terms. There were questions but never a *Gespräch* [conversation]. October to December 1922 the topic was "Urformen religiösen Lebens." In four sessions Buber dealt with magic, sacrifice, mystery, and prayer; the lectures were followed by seminars, "Zeugnisse Religiösen Lebens," dealing with selected texts from Egyptian, Babylonian, Indian, Persian, Syrian and Greek literatures, concluding with a discussion of Judaism and Christianity. The very diversity of readings made it impossible to present more than a rather superficial picture of religious thought.

Buber tried hard to establish a life contact with the students. At one point, while reading hasidic material, he asked his audience "to express itself" so that the seminar be more than the usual meeting of this kind and so that we may "counsel and help" each other — whereupon some of those present, and especially women, started to raise questions that were offensive in their "openness" and "directness." Buber smiled ironically but once, otherwise benevolently, not realizing that the meeting had deteriorated into a shameless performance. Ernst Simon, who attempted — in vain — to stop the "dialogue," wrote a critical letter to Buber (November 2, 1923) that remained unanswered.[31] Rosenzweig saw the draft of Simon's letter and somehow tried to understand Buber. I assume that Buber became a bit intimidated after this exchange.

The University at Frankfurt

In 1924 Buber received the invitation to represent Jewish religious thought and ethics at the University of Frankfurt, a position first offered to Rabbi N. A. Nobel, then, after his death in early 1922, to Rosenzweig. Rosenzweig accepted, though he knew that he wouldn't be able to teach; all he wanted was to secure for himself a voice in the selection of a successor. The position was unique, for it was the only one of its kind in Germany. Buber was the logical choice, though in the academic calendar he was listed as *Schriftsteller* [writer]. In the summer term of 1924 (April to August) he lectured on "Wie ist Religionswissenschaft möglich?" ["How is the scientific study of religion possible?"] The lectures were preceded by exercises (*übungen*) on Maimonides, *Hilchot Teshuvah* ("The Laws of Turning [to God]"). The enrollment was rather small, about fifteen students, if my memory does not fail me. The following term's topic (Winter 1924–25) was "Messianism," preceded by a seminar on messianic texts. Buber's style was heavy, labored, and often simply boring. He noticed the lack of attention on the part of the students and once asked me what could be done. I knew nothing better than to suggest to have an attendance sheet, read the names before the lecture, and recognize each student. He followed the advice, but he read the names with considerable detachment, so that the procedure was worthless. I attended all his lectures and seminars, took notes, and sometimes accompanied him after the lecture. This way he came to know me better. Later on, when he was "promoted" to *Honorar Professor* [unpaid adjunct professor] at the University, he recommended me as successor of his original lectureship in *Jüdische Religionswissenschaft und Ethic*. I held this appointment until the Nazis dismissed me, among other Jewish academics.

Corpus Hasidicum

In the early twenties Buber and Agnon conceived a plan of a *corpus hasidicum*, an encyclopedic handbook of hasidic sources. Buber asked me to assist them and I started the work, which was expected to occupy us several years. In a letter to Agnon, July 28, 1926, Buber mentions that "the copy that young Glatzer produced is very clean and in good order."[32] At some point the work came to a standstill; both Buber and Agnon found more worthwhile things to do.

Pharisäertum

In 1925 appeared Buber's essay "Das Pharisäertum" in the special issue of *Der Jude* dedicated to "Antisemitismus und Jüdisches Volkstum" [Antisemitism and Jewish Nationality]. I happened to be in Heppenheim at a working session with Buber when he was about to write this essay, which is a valiant defense of Pharisaism (against the usual Christian criticism). When the evening came I was shown my room and had a good night's sleep. In the morning I came down and found Buber at his desk as I had left him the night before. He spent the night writing this major article until it was completed. Or, perhaps he had a few hours sleep and got up early to finish the job.

Buber's study was filled with figures of saints; you could imagine yourself to be in a bishop's residence. Buber did not have the urge to consider the feelings of more conservative Jews who were surprised to find church art in the home of the great Jew.

Ponte Tresa

In the summer of 1928 the Swiss Buber group met in Ponte Tresa to study sessions around the topic The Biblical Concept of Kingdom; the basic text was the First Book of Samuel. It was my job to prepare the group for the text and lay the ground for Buber's interpretation. The work was most enjoyable. Among the participants were Dr. Haus Trüb, Dr. Marta Amrein, Steinbüchel (a judge), Dr. Lambert Schneider's wife, a very beautiful woman (who later committed suicide). Evenings were free, entertainment was provided by Dr. Josef Katzenstein, a German lawyer, who later gained some recognition as author of *Sabbatai Zevi* and a Jewish history (his name was then Josef Kastein). He had a deep voice and played the guitar. I was too shy to start talking to people, but as Buber wrote to Rosenzweig, some of the women fell in love with me (an unpublished letter). One day Buber met me when I was taking a walk in the neighborhood: "Are you contemplating the meaning of the boundary?"

In August 1929 my father was one of the victims of the Arabs' attack on Moza. Buber, who was then on one of his travels, wrote a card to Rosenzweig with this P.S.: "Please say to Glatzer that I greatly commiserate." I was sad that the man of "I and Thou" who knew me well did not think of writing to me but used Rosenzweig as his messenger. I never forgot that.

Optimism

Buber's optimism was boundless. He was able to recognize the existence of evil. In *For the Sake of Heaven*, he declared that evil is not "when I meet my fellowman ... I experience it when I meet myself."[33] And speaking of Gog, the enemy-king: "He can exist in the outer world only because he exists within us."[34]

At the end of the twenties, in a visit to Heppenheim, he brushed aside my apprehension that the Weimar Republic will be defeated by either the Communists or the Fascists and the world in which we live will come to an end. He did not consider the rise of Adolf Hitler as a decisive event, not even when, in the Presidential election of March 1932, Hitler won twice as many votes as the Communist Thälmann, and the constant disorders and clashes of rival groups indicated that a major change in the political structure was imminent. In August 1932 Hitler refused Hindenburg's request that he serve as vice-chancellor under von Papen and demanded "all or nothing."

Shortly before these events, Buber made the prognosis that no matter what changes may occur in the structure of the government, the Nazis will not possibly win the day. "As long as the present coalition lasts are real outrages against Jews or anti-Jewish legislation unthinkable. Only in the case of a switch of power in favor of the National Socialists could an anti-Jewish legislation come about — but this [switch] is not to be expected."[35]

In a letter to me (Anne and I left Germany at the end of March, 1933) from Zurich, April 24, 1933 Buber wrote, "Everything is unclear and I do not know for sure whether you did the right thing to leave."[36]

Buber remained in Germany, leading the cultural and educational efforts of the increasingly distressed Jewish community, until, in 1938, he was "advised" to leave the land of his mature activity.

Brandeis and Tillich

March 28, 1957 was Buber's second appearance at Brandeis. He insisted that the meeting be in the form of a colloquium, restricted to about twenty-five students. That restriction proved to be impossible to keep. My telephone rang all the time, people attempting to be invited. Abraham Maslow, for example, wanted to observe the gestures of Buber, important to him as a psychologist. Paul Tillich of Harvard wanted to participate in such a theological colloquium with Buber. The evening turned out to be a discussion on the use of concepts. Buber opposed the use of concepts as a hindrance to direct, immediate speech. Tillich stressed the usefulness of concepts as a means to simplify our speech. Buber descended from the podium which we had erected for him, approached Tillich (who sat in the first row), shook him by the lapel, as if to bring him to his senses; use as little concepts as absolutely necessary; if we have to sin, let us sin as little as necessary. The evening ended; Buber (and I) stood outside the student union; in a while Tillich came out and Buber turned to him: "Tillich, Sie haben noch viel zu lernen" (Tillich, you still have much to learn).

I and Thou

Are Buber's teachings of the I-Thou relationship and response, immediacy and spontaneity – are these records of personal experience, or rather records of expectation and longing anticipation? Buber himself speaks on several occasions of deeply meaningful personal encounters. There is also ample evidence of misunderstandings, which a man of Buber's sensitivity must have taken as signs of rejection, of failure to grasp the outstretched hand.

This notion can now be radically revised. True, I and Thou was for decades a rarely realized vision, a dream of an ideal interpersonal realm. But in the very last period of his life, the old man was rewarded for clinging steadfastly to the hope for encounter. Almost miraculously a human heart began beating for him, a loving voice spoke to him, and the words spoken should not be given the formal term "dialogue." Simplicity, immediacy, frankness, openness, of which he spoke and wrote in the course of a long life, now became pure, genuine, childlike presence. The famous man savored the taste, the smell, the touch of life in its most basic forms.

Those close to him resented this turn in Buber's life. To him it was fulfillment; at last. I and Thou became real, a warm, intimate, blissful event.

At one time in his later years he was asked point blank: Do you pray? He took a sheet of paper and wrote (in German): Prayer before going to sleep: "Into thy hand I commend my spirit." Prayer after awakening: "I thank thee, living and lasting King, that thou hast returned to me my soul with compassion. Great is thy faithfulness."

(The first is indeed a quotation from the prayer before retiring at night; the second is the start of the morning prayer for children.)

Anecdote

During the siege of Jerusalem in 1948 Buber took some time off from his work and entered a coffee house to have his favored drink (which was coffee). In came a man in civilian garb and seated himself at Buber's table. The two started to talk – of course about the city and its precarious situation. There was no knowing whether Jerusalem will be able to survive the siege. Buber took out a piece of paper and sketched out the strategic position of the city and the possibilities of defense should the Arabs make this offensive or that, and what to do to secure the transport of provisions for both the army and the civilian population. The other man listened intently, made a remark here and there and asked pertinent questions, which Buber answered, like a man who knows his stuff.

Later it turned out that the other man was the commander of Jerusalem, who slipped into civilian clothing and allowed himself a short break from the arduous task of defending the city.

Buber and Rosenzweig as Bible Translators

These were the years 1925 to 1929 when the two threw all their energies into the unique translation of Scriptures into German. The original idea came from Lambert Schneider, an unconventional, enterprising young Christian Berlin publisher with a special interest in modern Judaica; soon he was to join forces with the Schocken firm. Schneider turned to Buber with the translation idea. Buber accepted, providing Franz Rosenzweig would participate in the venture. Rosenzweig knew that he would never see the completion of the work, but agreed while stipulating that the title pages carry the phrase, "a translation undertaken by M.B. and F.R." "Undertaken" – not more.

Their first idea was to bring Luther up-to-date to correct inaccuracies and to watch out for texts where Luther's Christianity shines through ("wo die Schrift Christian treibet"). A sample chapter convinced the two of the futility of an attempt to revise Luther. Luther is a majestic monument of German literature and should not be revised. They saw no alternative to starting "from the beginning" in the true sense of the word. A procedure was agreed upon that Buber would make the first draft of a section or chapter, mail it to Rosenzweig, who would note down his proposed changes (or questions) in a copy book (where the original pages could be ripped out and mailed, while retaining a carbon copy in the book). Buber would then react to these remarks or suggestions and, if necessary, send in new queries to Rosenzweig. What was left as not agreed upon was discussed in editorial meetings when the two met in Rosenzweig's study. As a rule the meetings took place on Wednesday afternoon and lasted for several hours into the evening; Buber then took a late train back to Heppenheim. More than once it happened that Buber felt tired and suggested that the meeting be ended. Rosenzweig, who had more reason to be tired, looked pleadingly at Buber, meaning, let us continue a little longer; it is a pity to interrupt the work. I do not remember who of the two gave in. Mrs. Rosenzweig, who sat at her husband's side and helped him to move his finger on the ABC tablet, had a most tiring job to do and was glad when the strenuous day came to an end.

I was asked to be "the first reader," who would carefully examine the proof galleys, watching for omissions, inconsistencies, lack of clarity, useful interpretations found in classical Hebrew commentaries, and simple linguistic issues. The two dealt with the questions thus raised and, if found of value, made a change in the translation.

While they were discussing issues I used to make quick notes for later reference. Here are some of the notes:

Buber, in a general discussion on the Book Leviticus: "I work much with my imagination." When I proposed a simpler rendition for Leviticus 26:13, Buber defended his and Rosenzweig's: "Ours is too beautiful and something should be done for it." When after a long discussion a satisfactory translation was found for Numbers 10:3, said Buber: "Now it's good; one must labor hard (*roboten muss man*)." When I objected to a too literal rendition of Numbers 10:3 where all the pecularities of the Hebrew text were transposed into German, Buber, a bit angry: "Should I offer a prize if you can make it better? But first you must see all the difficulties!" Rosenzweig to Buber, referring to a previous discussion of this passage: "The bridge collapses!" Buber: "I knew, this translation will be our undoing!" The artfully contrived rendition remained.

They discussed Numbers 16:33, where Rosenzweig pressed for a more literal translation; Buber interrupted his friend and turned very seriously to him and to me: "You contribute to the de-Germanization of the text," alluding to the subtitle of the work: Scripture undertaken to de-Germanize by ... (reading *ent-deutschen* for *verdeutschen*).[37] Another time I remarked that the all too literal translation of Numbers 21:26 would result in an annoying rhyme, whereupon Buber explained: "I did it out of my love for imperfection; you must have noticed that Rosenzweig loves perfection; I love imperfection." Buber, referring to Rosenzweig's philosophical accuracy: "He remembers the whole story; I keep forgetting!" Or, "I am lighthearted; he is not lighthearted." When I objected to the insertion of the word "thus" (*so*) in Numbers 22:22 (as not corresponding to the text though making the text more plausible), Buber remarked: "One has to do something on behalf of theology." Again, objecting to a suggested rendition of mine: "Doesn't work; you can go break your neck." On the Book of Judges: "Nothing but tricks; the text is completely corrupt. Yes, we have come to the rescue. We are a rescue organization." [38]

Rosenzweig died December 10, 1929 after completing the work on the Book of Isaiah. In re-reading the chapters on the suffering servant, he broke into tears.

Remarkable is that neither Buber nor Rosenzweig were biblical scholars in the exact, technical sense of the term. They had a deep interest in the Bible, in biblical life and faith. What they brought to their work was their training as scholars, in scholarly method, in the history of religion, and their sensitivity to language and style. Long ago, Rosenzweig was attracted to making translations from the Hebrew; he rendered into German e.g., the *Grace After Meals,* the home liturgy for Friday evenings and the Festivals. Buber rewrote, paraphrased hasidic stories adapting the at times crude style of the originals to an elegant, appealing German. But both men realized that the Bible called for a very different treatment: the supreme command was a strict adherence to the text (and the context).

When *Isaiah* appeared not long after Rosenzweig's death, Buber had the publisher insert a note informing the public of the nature of Rosenzweig's contribution. A parenthetical statement declared that Rosenzweig mailed to him, Buber, critical notes and proposed changes to the individual sections of his, Buber's, manuscripts. When I met Buber next (in my apartment, discussing critically the continuation of the Bible work), I blamed him for making the above statement on Rosenzweig, obviously with the intention to minimize Rosenzweig's part in the enterprise. Buber objected and repeated that that was indeed the procedure —"don't you know this?" Of course I knew, but since Rosenzweig did not publicize his impairment and rather underplayed it whenever it became known, I felt it was not right to reduce his part in the work to providing critical notes, while creating the impression that the main portion was Buber's. Also, in this connection, the timing was wrong ("right" only for practical reasons). This criticism came unexpectedly to Buber. I never forgot this overly "practical" procedure.

Franz Kafka

How did I discover him? By chance, if there is such a thing. I was on my way somewhere in Frankfurt and, unexpectedly, met Fritz Millner coming from the other direction. He was carrying a book under his arm. "What is that?" I asked. Franz Kafka's *Der Prozess*; you must read it. That was 1925 or 1926, shortly after the book's publication. I read the novel and then whatever else was available. Kurt Wolff had published a number of Kafka pamphlets: *Das Urteil, Die Verwandlung, Der Heizer.* I bought a whole supply of these booklets and used them for presents for all occasions. What drew me to Kafka was his uncanny penetration into the human condition. In speaking of the vermin, of the old father, the ambiguous son, the land surveyor, K the accused one, the boy on his way to America — it is always yourself he is talking about.

About twenty years after my "discovery" of Kafka, I became technically involved in the act of bringing his writings to the attention of the English-reading public. One of the first projects of the newly founded Schocken Books in New York (1945) was the English edition of Kafka's Diaries. The work had not yet appeared in the German original and the English version had to be based on Max Brod's typescript, or rather on a typescript of the diaries edited by Max Brod. It was my privilege to share in the editorial work and in the supervision of the translation into English. Here an "editorial note" must be added. The ever vigilant, ever suspicious, ever circumspect Mr. Salman Schocken, before the war broke out, had prevailed upon Brod to deposit the Kafka manuscripts into his, Schocken's, fireproof safe in his library; the key was to be in Brod's hands. But sometime between the deposit of the manuscripts in the safe and the handing-in of the key, Schocken had the material quickly photographed. So that the New York editors had at their disposal both Brod's version of the diaries and a faithful photo of Kafka originals.

What was possibly an unethical procedure (the unauthorized photography of the Kafka manuscripts) turned out to be a boon as far as the loyalty to Kafka's work and editorial accuracy was concerned. For, indeed,

Brod had not only adjusted the punctuation and spelling to the current usage and helped with the transcription of Czech names, but made changes in the text, designed to rescue Kafka's reputation and preserve his greatness. I remember one example: At one point Kafka exclaimed: "How I envy Werfel." Brod omitted that naive reference to Franz Werfel, who had enjoyed something like fame in his time to be well nigh forgotten as years went by. Brod omitted this sentence. We at Schocken of course restored the phrase, not only because it adds rather than detracts from Kafka's humanity, but also for the sake of editorial accuracy. The German publication, based on Brod's transcript, appeared shortly after the English edition; it was strangely enough (but not strangely to us) less faithful than the English version. Brod, informed of the "discrepancies," was furious, but had no leg to stand on.

Other works of Kafka were translated into English; most successful were the collections of short stories, *The Great Wall of China* (1946),[39] *Dearest Father* (1954) (Brod's typescript said "Lieber Vater," while Kafka's script had clearly "Liebter Vater"),[40] *Description of a Struggle* (1958).[41]

Hannah Arendt was asked to edit a collection of Kafka's *Parables*, a bilingual edition. Later on I was assigned the preparation of an expanded edition; it appeared under the title *Parables and Paradoxes* (1961). Independent of my choice, the same title was chosen by Heinz Politzer for his projected Kafka book. He asked me to change my title but Herzl Rome advised me not to retreat. Both books appeared; no one was bothered by the titles.

As I read Kafka over and over again, I asked myself whether there may be one particular literary motif that occupied Kafka's mind more than others. I hit upon the Tree of Knowledge motif that occurs many times in his aphorisms. At some point he says (without boasting) that he believes to understand more than others what the "Fall" really means. His remarks on the Tree of Knowledge versus the Tree of Life probe deeply into the universally human implication of the story. Knowledge implies awareness of death and is, therefore, the contrasting force to "Life" and the naive, unquestioned, animal-like, paradisical enjoyment thereof. You cannot have both. The decision to appropriate Knowledge is paid for by the exclusion from the Tree of Life, i.e. the expulsion from Paradise. Man is an exile and cannot return; yet, more tragic than the expulsion from Paradise would have been the destruction of the Paradise; that this happened is not reported.

It was clear to me that these reflections were basic to Kafka's world view. When I made this "discovery" I thought this understanding of Life (good) and Knowledge (dangerous, death-directed) on the part of Kafka is the ground (conscious or not) of most of his stories. I wrote it down in an essay "Franz Kafka and the Tree of Knowledge" (*Between East and West,* a volume in memory of Bela Horovitz, 1958),[42] but nobody paid attention and Kafka bibliographies did not notice the article.

Ted Schocken invited me to prepare two Kafka volumes: a new edition of Kafka's complete stories with bibliographical and other appendices, and an intellectual biography of Kafka, culled as much as possible from the author's own autobiographical writings, especially from his diaries. I started to work on the second project by marking up copies of the diaries and letters, especially those that appeared in the German *Briefe.* The work fascinated me for I saw in it an opportunity to present Kafka's life in his own words. He mentions more than once that he would have liked to write an autobiography and some critics say that all of Kafka's writings are autobiographical. I steered clear of this extreme position and adhered to what is beyond doubt biographical. The fact that Kafka destroyed parts of his diaries was rather painful to realize; in such cases letters helped, but they were a poor substitute.

I wanted the volume to be called: "F.K.'s Life ... presented by ...". Beverly Colman in the Schocken office insisted that it should read "edited by," which gave the impression that Kafka left behind actual autobiographical writings that merely required an editorial job. I was in Los Angeles at the time; I wrote to explain the difference between the two, but did not succeed to convince. I should not have given in; later I regretted it. But even with "edited by ... ," I expected greater success. Only one reviewer said, "This is the nearest thing to an autobiography that we will ever get."

Before I started to work on the "autobiography," Ted mentioned the project to Marianne Steiner (Kafka's niece) in London, a highly sensitive and insightful lady. She must have said a few friendly things about me to Ted to win him over for what she had on her heart. She was, she told Ted, apprehensive that I would make Franz appear "too Jewish." Ted must have put her at ease but I don't believe she was entirely convinced. What a shameful attitude. Since there is so much Jewishness in Kafka — both on the surface and deeply hidden, a Judaism the relevance of which is at once affirmed and doubted, a Judaism forgotten yet over and over again recalled into a brightly shining memory – to disregard this realm in fear the gentiles may be displeased would be dishonesty, falsification of Kafka's life.

The title of the book is taken from Kafka's notes, *I Am A Memory Come Alive.* The wise will understand, in the words of Abraham ibn Ezra.

The editorial preparation of the English edition of *Letters to Friends, Family, and Editors* required a lot of work; Richard and Clara Winston's translation needed close attention, for their German was far from perfect. I sat back and answered editorial questions and watched over the footnotes and the Judaic references. The book appeared in 1977.[43]

The annual editorial meetings of the international board for the critical edition of Kafka's work goes on. The main archives are in Wuppertal. The main difficulty is the fact that the only manuscript of *Prozess* ("The Trial") is in the possession of Esther Hoffe of Tel Aviv and she makes impossible conditions – with a veto right in all matters for the use of the manuscript. Lawyers of Fischer-Verlag talk to the lawyer of Frau Hoffe – exactly as Kafka would have wanted. At one point Frau Hoffe tried to smuggle the manuscript out of Israel and was caught by the Israeli customs officers. Somehow she won the right to transport the *Prozess* to Zurich.

Another difficulty is connected with the name Hartmut Binder. He is a good Kafka scholar, though a bit too much statistically oriented.[44] He managed to extract from Brod some important information regarding Kafka and some Kafka material from Schocken. He promised Schocken not to use the material so as not to jeopardize the historical-critical edition. He did not keep his promise and published some hitherto unknown material – always giving credit so that no one can say he acted illegally. This makes some portions of the planned edition superfluous. My suggestion (twice) was to take him into the editorial group and let him participate in its activity. Malcolm Pasley opposed that suggestion most vehemently and threatened to resign. Paul Raabe agreed with me; no decision was taken, but nobody wants to antagonize Pasley, one of the most valuable men on the committee. With reference to my position at the editorial board, Binder calls me "die graue Eminenz."

F.B.

Felice Bauer, Kafka's fiancée; but originally Max Brod saw to it that "the world" should not know the true name and learn to stand in awe before these initials. I remember how thrilled I was to be informed of the "name."

And then, after years, that Mrs. Marasse (her name after marriage) appeared at Schocken Books with the package of letters by Kafka to negotiate Schocken's acquisition of the letters and the right to publish them. It was my task to conduct the initial stages of the negotiation. For F.B. wanted to see the letters published, and at the same time wanted to keep them to herself. I pointed to the importance of F.K. in the world of literature and of her contribution if she would release the letters. I was struck by the ugliness of her face and the commonness of its expression and could not imagine that she was attractive as a young woman, outside of the natural advantage that youth has. Well, K. must have realized it, for in recording the first time he met her (at Max Brod's home), she appeared to him like a "Dienstmädchen"— a phrase Brod tried to eliminate from the first German edition of the *Diaries* (which he edited). She got all excited when the talk turned to the greatness of F.K. "Mein Franz war ein Heiliger (My Franz was a saint)," she said repeatedly, and then inquired about the whereabouts of Odradek, forgetting that this is an imaginary figure in a story.[45] She reenacted the final farewell with Franz, which must have been the saddest event in F.B.'s life. She pictured the hand of Kafka stretching across the room until she was right out of sight. Finally she was ready to sell and release the letters with some serious reservations which I could not deal with. Here Mr. S. Schocken took over and, if I remember correctly, referred to a package of letters by Grete Bloch that he had effectfully placed on his desk. He told her quite openly that he would publish these letters by her friend and, as far as F.K. was concerned, her serious rival, unless she takes back her reservation. I believe the reservations concerned a small collection of Kafka's letters which she considered most intimate and which should not be published while she was alive – or something of the kind.

The *Briefe an Felice* appeared in 1967; the volume contained also the Grete Bloch letters – not as an appendix but in chronological order with the Felice letters.[46] Erich Heller and Jürgen Born, the editors, in their introduction to the first Grete letter, argued against the possibility that she, Grete, was the mother of Kafka's son (of which Kafka knew nothing) but the fact that some (including Max Brod and Klaus Wagenbach) assume this motherhood of Grete is at least recorded.

I believe it, for Wolfgang Schocken showed me Grete Bloch's letter where she talks about the event without, however, mentioning F.K. by name. I asked Schocken (no relation to the publisher) whether there is any chance of an erroneous assumption or a distortion of facts. He, who knew her well, denied it. So we are left with two women and the only F.K.

Salman Schocken

In about 1926, Ludwig Strauss prepared for the projected Schocken Verlag an anthology of modern Jewish writing when the thought occurred that a Jewish anthology should start with the classical period. It must have been Buber who recommended me to Salman Schocken as a Hebraist to assist Ludwig Strauss in the composition of such a volume (which was to be followed by the modern part as volume 5). I received the commission and a fee of 200 Marks per month — a turn of events which made me quite happy: it gave me a chance to work on a book and to have a fixed salary. Soon it developed that I had to do most of the work: selection of the material, making a first draft of the translation, checking Strauss's suggested revisions, annotation. We used to meet once a week, in Beusheim, where he lived at the time. I did not mind the work; I loved it and, of course, appreciated Strauss's exquisite German style. Schocken received information on the progress of the work. Once the manuscript was completed, Schocken took considerable interest in the production of the book, which he wanted to be technically and aesthetically perfect. It appeared (1931) as the first work in the new Schocken Verlag under the high-sounding title *Sendung und Schicksal* ("Mission and Fate"), with an appropriate subtitle. It established me as a Judaic writer and led to further assignments.

When Anne and I married (January 1931), we planned to pay Schocken a visit in St. Moritz on our way to Palestine. I was not surprised to confront a highly intelligent and cultured man, interested in many things outside his own field. We spent a few very stimulating hours and I was glad he had a chance to know me personally. I mentioned we were on our honeymoon and he asked, "How long have you been married?" I said, "Three days," which I thought sounded better than "two days," which was the truth. I don't think he noticed my embarrassment. In parting he handed me 200 Marks to be given to a needy person in the Holy Land. According to Jewish belief, "a messenger who is going to perform a good deed cannot be harmed." A meaningful tenet. In Palestine I gave anonymously 100 Marks each to two needy Jewish writers. And I remembered Schocken's generosity for many years. He could be generous, but also stingy, too; friendly and rude; affectionate and hostile.

When the Nazis took over his department stores in Germany before letting him leave the land, he came to Palestine and, according to the report of a friend, declared:"Now I am a poor man." If I remember correctly the friend's information, the poverty consisted of £200,000. That is how relative things are.

I continued working for the Verlag ... Schocken discussed a number of plans; his intention was to create in Germany an internal defense against Nazi barbarism, something that would guard the Jewish soul from within. He did not fail.

Nineteen thirty-eight brought a threat of war and in 1939 the war started. Palestine was in dire peril and I wanted to believe that it was better for us and for little Daniel to stay away. Then immediately after the end of the war, Salman Schocken came to the United States, visited Chicago (his relative Fritz Kaufmann lived there), and assembled a few people to discuss the chance for the establishment of a new Jewish publishing house in America. Soon the plan matured and (in 1945) Schocken Books Inc. was established in New York. Max Strauss, brother of Ludwig and an early translator of Agnon, was appointed editor, and my services, mainly as a writer, were added.

Schocken's original idea was to acquire all existing publishing firms of Judaica, retain from their list what is of high caliber and culturally relevant, remainder the rest (i.e, most of the titles) and start a new program of highest standard Judaica and translations from the Hebrew (mainly of the classical period) — a program which would have in effect initiated a Jewish intellectual renaissance. The firms resisted and, naturally, wished to retain their vested interests. Schocken did not expect such strong opposition, but had to face the facts and gave up the great plan.

The alternative plan was to examine the German Schocken titles to determine what could be introduced to the American Jewish market. For this Schocken worked out a long memo where he remarked on each title, giving his views on what could be taken over and what revisions were necessary. In this memo occurred the memorable phrase:"Hier haben wir es zum ersten Mal mit einem lebenden Autor zu tun"(Here for the first time do we encounter a living author), which meant, trouble was to be expected. The best author is a dead author, a living one is a nuisance, at least. This memo of course, was meant for internal consumption only.

A first project was to be an English version of *Sendung und Schicksal*. I tried to adapt the material to what I believed to be the American Jewish mentality and receptivity for classical Judaic sources. I confess that I did not know enough for the job. Olga Marx Perlzweig did the translation (from the German) and I checked this against the Hebrew original. The book (appeared 1946) was rather well received and reviewed (especially by Ludwig Lewisohn), and in the course of time sold rather well, especially in the paperback edition. The original title of the American edition *In Time and Eternity: A Jewish Reader* was changed for the paperback issue and only the subtitle remained: *A Jewish Reader.* Simple. Mr. Salman Schocken was pleased with the venture and that was important.

At first I commuted between Boston (where I taught at Hebrew Teachers College, 1943 to 1947) and New York, to take care of the editorial end of Schocken Books. The publishing activity grew and Schocken offered me a full time job as chief editor if I transferred to New York. We decided to move to New York. Schocken helped us to get a beautiful apartment at 135 Eastern Parkway, Brooklyn; the "living room" was turned into a magnificent study. On certain days I worked at home, especially in the period when Agnon's *Days of Awe* was being prepared (with the help of Jacob Sloan, the English stylist).

It was challenging to work for Schocken. His perfectionism appealed to me. The story was told that when his son Michael finished his technical training and produced his "masterpiece," a lock, he proudly showed it to his father. "Very nice, very nice," exclaimed the father, while focusing his one healthy eye intently on the one spot of the lock that was not so "very nice." This criticism did not remain unnoticed.

His stubbornness is well known. An early evidence was his reaction to the Dresdener Bank which, as he told me, refused to grant him and his brother a loan to expand their business. Not enough security, said the bank. So be it, said Schocken, and decided never to make use of banks. The business grew tremendously without the bank's support. How a business can do without the use of a bank (where do you keep your money?) I do not know, but I am sure the stubborn Schocken kept his word. He even founded his own insurance company to protect his employees – and his own interest.

He loved Goethe and a few more select German classics and always travelled with a few volumes of especially leather-bound works on thin paper and practically without margins, just to save precious space. Once it happened that he had to take a night flight. Mrs. Regina Klapper, an important co-worker at the publishing house, brought him to the airport. Mr. Schocken was tired, the hour was late; the old man sank more and more into himself and got Mrs. Klapper worried. Finally the plane took off. Some hours later, in the darkness of the night, Mrs. Klapper's telephone rang. The first thought that occurred to her was that something terrible must have happened to Mr. Schocken. Nothing of the kind. "Here is Mr. Schocken, I forgot on my desk volume so and so of Goethe. Please mail it to me the first thing in the morning." Is commentary needed?

Another time Mrs. Klapper brought Mr. Schocken to the airport and there was still some time before departure. "Mrs. Klapper, please take some notes." The notes referred to an imaginary reconstruction of the airport; which passage to be expanded, which walls broken down to make room for this or that, where to place the ticket counters, and so on. His constructive mind could not rest and so for an imaginary while the airport became his concern; it mattered little that, practically speaking, the notes were more than useless.

He wanted to be treated as the one and only Mr. Schocken. Once he wanted to visit a certain exhibition at the Jewish Museum (I think it was Abraham Walkowitz) and was informed that the exhibit was closed and the paintings removed from the walls. Never mind, said Schocken to the curator, have them brought up from wherever they are. Some consternation. But the paintings (or some of them) were brought back and Mr. Schocken given his chance to see the stuff. Then he thanked them and left.

Once he did not feel like waiting at the airport and had Mrs. Klapper announce at the ticket counter that here was an elderly and unwell person that should be allowed to board the plane first. This was done, of course, and Mr. Schocken could install himself in his seat before "the masses" stormed in. But the considerate airline went a step further. When the plane landed in Zurich and Mr. Schocken was allowed to be the first to deplane he noticed to his dismay that a sick chair was waiting at the foot of the steps and he guessed for whom the chair was. It happened that he was to be met at the gate by a noble lady friend and, quite naturally, did not want to arrive as a cripple. He nervously waived the chair and the attendant away so that he could arrive at the gate as a well rested, alert and sprightly looking gentleman, ready to give a lady a good time.

He knew the role of the scholar, the intellectual, the artist in society, but a higher state was the one of the practical man, the man of direct action. At the time when he tried to tie me closer to the publishing firm, he asked me: "Schämen Sie sich nicht, ein Professor zu sein?" (Are you not ashamed to be a professor?) No, I was rather proud to be one, but knowing Mr. Schocken I at least understood what he meant.

Discussing his sons he pointed to the achievements of each one, except Gideon. "He is just a general." Perhaps he did not mean it. He appreciated the genius of Franz Kafka and the great gifts of Agnon, whom he discovered early in the twenties. He had a sense for Rosenzweig, more than for Buber, whom he cultivated mainly because he was a well-known man. He was critical of Buber's theatrics. He told the story how the two were once lodging together; Buber was preparing an address he was to deliver. He wrote the text, then by reading it over had it committed to memory. But when he delivered the speech the audience was made to believe that the speaker was struggling over the ideas as they came to him at the moment, that he was coining the beautiful phrases, that the quotations and allusions just occurred to him at the moment. He paused for moments of reflection, placed his hand to his large forehead to help the flow of ideas, etc. But everything was planned in advance, the text, the phrases, the quotations, the allusions, the spontaneity, and the inspiration. If this is theater, it is at least good theater.

Schocken, by contrast, wrote with the greatest of difficulties. The sentences had to be short; no superfluous word could be used. Negatives had to be avoided. There were numerous revisions and rewrites until Schocken was satisfied. When Leo Baeck's *The Pharisees and Other Essays* was to be published with a "publisher's note," all that was allowed to stand was that Baeck was "a representative of German Jewry."[47] It did not bother Schocken that a thousand others were equally "representative." He was deeply convinced that a book or an essay speaks for itself; there is no need to "sell" the author. Thus he sternly interfered with my "Zwischentexte" (transitional passages) in my *Franz Rosenzweig: His Life and Thought.* "Give just the dates, don't explain." I resented his approach at the time. Schocken did not expect the book to be accepted by the public. He proposed that I contact a number of public figures, including rabbis, get from them an advance reaction and preferably an order, and proceed only once a sufficient number of affirmative statements were secured. I resisted this humiliating procedure. Ernst Simon, who was in the United States at the time, was consulted on the prospect of the manuscript (which in the meanwhile was completed). He — rightly — thought the first, biographical, part will appeal to the reader while the second part, an anthology from Rosenzweig's writings, will not. The first part was indeed of considerable impact while the second was read as an intelligent introduction to the man's work. The book found its place in this country beyond what I could imagine. Very many rabbinical students, Conservative and Reform, read the book as pointing a new way to Judaism, or way beyond Orthodoxy and Liberalism. The story of the Day of Atonement 1913 became a myth signifying the converting power of authentic Judaism. Only a few years ago Raphael and Rachel Rosenzweig started a "campaign" to question the historical accuracy of the event as described in the book, based on information supplied by Mrs. Adele Rosenzweig, Franz's mother.[48]

Schocken placed considerable stress on the "Schocken library" project, patterned after the German "Schocken Bücherei." Here he wanted to create a library of the essential books of Judaism, ancient, classical and modern. Uniformly produced, 128 pages each volume, Schocken expected a major breakthrough to the heart and mind of modern, intelligent Jewish readers. He brushed aside my cautious criticism. Volume one was *Language of Faith: A Selection of Jewish Prayers*, issued together with volumes numbered two to five in 1947. I made the selection, arrangement and annotation, and Jacob Sloan translated most of the material; there was a certain novelty and freshness in these translations. In the selection I followed my instinct for the genuine expression of faith.

If this is an indication of acceptance by the reader: this volume one — that Schocken in a publisher's preface called "a dedication of intention" of his publishing enterprise — was the first among the 20 volumes to reach the sales figure of 5,000 and go out of print.

About twenty years later, T. Herzl Rome,[49] who after Salman Schocken's death became the head of the firm, proposed a second, expanded edition of the *Language of Faith*. I put much love and energy into this project; the new edition was richer in content, and very beautiful in form; the *ot shocken*, the Schocken Hebrew lettering, was used with a corresponding old Latin lettering. The completed volume was a joy to handle and a happy experience to read. But the book failed to attract the reader and all sales tricks were of no avail. My sneaking feeling is that in the course of twenty years the number of those who would appreciate (if not read) the Hebrew typeface diminished greatly and the Hebrew text on the facing page was a waste of paper and of money. Perhaps a collection in English only would have been a more reasonable approach. (Such an edition appeared in 1974; it was a failure.)

Buber's *Tales of the Hasidim*, first *The Early Masters*, then *The Later Masters*, was based on Buber's newly edited *Chassidische Geschichten*. Olga Marx Perlzweig translated the German material without knowing anything about hasidic lore and the world from which Hasidism emerged. It was a job to see that justice was done to this background. Despite the errors and oversights, *The Tales* made a deep impression on the reader. (By the way, Buber saw the translation and sent in corrections; but his English was not very satisfactory for the job.)

Schocken invited Hannah Arendt to join the firm as an editor for non-Judaica, and especially for Kafka. She and I were co-ordinated as chief editors but she tried to assert her superiority — which I did not mind. A typescript of Kafka's *Diaries* was prepared and supplied by Max Brod and the German text was translated into English; it was to be published before the German text went into production.

Willy Haas sent in Kafka's letters to Milena. Schocken worked diligently on the sequence because the letters were not dated. To this day (1973) the matter of sequence is a problem in Kafka research. The English version came out in 1953;[50] critics immediately realized the great beauty of this collection.

Among the first projects of the American house was an English edition of the A.D. Goldschmidt *Passover Haggadah*; the German edition had appeared in the Schocken Bücherei. It was of no value to reproduce the vast scholarly apparatus. On the other hand, Schocken's charge to me, "Address the English version to the dentist" was too drastic to be taken at face value. Does the dentist need a Passover Haggadah (beyond his possible desire to gain a better understanding of the phrase, "set his teeth on edge")? So I tried to steer a course between scholarship and popularization. What is the background of the text and how did the text grow and change?

The Haggadah was published only in 1953, when Schocken had entered an unholy alliance with Farrar, Strauss.[51] That my name appears on the title page (as editor) is due to Anne, who insisted that that was my right; I yielded without conviction. The Haggadah appeared in several reprints; Holocaust material was added.

My whole heart was in the *Midrash Reader*, which Gideon Schocken helped to name *Hammer on the Rock*, in an allusion to a midrashic expression of verse in Jeremiah [23:29]. The selection was restricted to 128 pages of a library volume while my plan was to have a representative anthology of aggadic literature three times the size.[52]

A good example of a splendid idea of Mr. Schocken that, however, led to nothing is the Jewish History Outlines. This was supposed to follow the example of Langer's *Outlines of History* (which has very little references to Jewish history). The project was first suggested to Henry Fischel, who had done the *First Book of Maccabees* for Schocken (the commentary was largely a borrowing from C. H. Charles, *Apocrypha*). Fischel thought a long while and finally rejected it. After a few more disappointments, I took on the project and produced some sample chapters. The book would have covered the whole width and breadth of Jewish history and literature. After years of revising and rewritings went by, I finally realized that the whole thing was beyond my powers and that errors would be plenty; I would have to rely on many secondary treatments without the ability to check every detail. I gave up and limited myself to using my material for my Jewish history courses at Brandeis.

Another work that was close to Schocken's heart was Ismar Elbogen's *History of Jewish Liturgy*. Kurt Wilhelm had years ago done a first revision of the German text; I took up the job and marked up a copy for the use of the translator. There were several unsuccessful attempts to translate the work – the last one was by Mrs. Chaim Rabin – until the Elbogen family had to be informed that as far as Schocken was concerned, it could not be done. The perfection, or at least the exactness, that Schocken required caused that a number of good projects were started and then abandoned, while on the market appeared second- and third-rate books, badly edited and badly produced.

I often had the notion that at times Schocken wanted to talk to me about personal matters, but I must have given him the impression that I would rather avoid such subjects. When Schocken got a separation (or a divorce) from his wife, he started the agenda of the day saying, "Now I am a free man" (*Jetzt bin ich frei*). Free for what? Once I asked him how he explained the fact that Kafka had several affairs while engaged to marry F.B. Schocken was pleased to respond, "An artist needs finger exercises."

A.S.Yahuda, Egyptologist

Abraham Shalom Yahuda was born in Jerusalem, in 1872. The family traced its origin back to the Geonim of Babylonia and to great scholars and community leaders in Spain. His father, Rabbi Benjamin, emigrated to Jerusalem from Baghdad and married a daughter of Eliezer Bergmann. This Bergmann came to Jerusalem in 1834 with his wife Rivka Zylla, who was one of the daughters of Reb Mendel Rosenbaum of Zell (near Wurzburg, in Bavaria), a spokesman of Jewry in his region and its representative before the court of King Maximilian II. The Reb Mendel of Zell, famous for his great piety and good deeds, is one of Anne's ancestors. Our children were early made aware of this fact; a picture of his likeness hangs in my study.

Abraham Shalom received the traditional Jewish education, but was allowed to go abroad to acquire the wisdom of the world. At one point — was it before the inception of formal study? — he was sent to Frankfurt, where his "family" was expected to look after him. Naturally, he conformed to the lifestyle of the family, observing the Sabbath, the dietary laws, etc. It is reported (by a distant member of the family) that one Sabbath morning young Abraham felt an irresistible urge to smoke a cigarette. Since he knew he could not commit such a sin in Frankfurt, he went to the railroad station and took a train to Fürth (or one of the other provincial cities near Frankfurt) and started to indulge in the frivolous act of smoking on the holy day. It may well be that it was not the cigarette he craved but the freedom [to] break the Jewish law. It did not take long and he was approached by someone unknown to him. "What are you doing here, Herr Yahuda?" It was a member of the "family" in Frankfurt who chanced to be in Fürth (or wherever). The news spread in Frankfurt that the son of the Orient is but an *apikores** who is not ashamed to smoke on the Sabbath. From then on he was rejected by the clan; there was only one family that had pity on him and made a further stay in Frankfurt possible.

The precocious youngster took the incident in his stride. He was convinced of his real worth. After all, the only fifteen-year-old boy had — in

*Colloqial for heretic

1893 – published his first book, *Kadmoniyot ha-Aravim* ("Arab Antiquities").

To study Semitic languages, Yahuda went to the Universities of Heidelberg and Strasbourg. At the latter he was a pupil of the famous Theodor Noeldecke. In 1904 Yahuda received his doctoral degree and in 1905 was invited to teach Semitic philology at the Hochschule (later Lehranstalt) für die Wissenschaft des Judentums in Berlin, a liberal rabbinical school, and at the Orientalisches Seminar at the Berlin University. At the time, the leaders of the Berlin Jewish community (a rather stuffy and respectable body mainly of businessmen and lawyers) planned a formal reception for the emperor William II. One of the major synagogues (Fasanenstrasse on the Kurfürstendamm) was fittingly prepared and the program worked out in all detail. Legend has it that Professor Yahuda was invited as a guest of the community for, it was thought, he might lend luster and some prestige to the occasion. When he was presented to the emperor – all according to legend – he stepped forward, addressing himself to the ruler: "May I address a word to your majesty?" The emperor nodded (while the community leaders looked at each other in apprehension) and Yahuda (referring to the unwritten law that a Jewish couple, at marriage, had to acquire a certain amount of tiles [the so-called *Kadiner Kacheln*] from a royal factory) continued: "Does you majesty appreciate the difference between the Pharaohs of Egypt and yourself? In Egypt the Israelites made bricks for Pharaoh, while in Prussia, your majesty makes bricks for the Israelites." If the emperor got the joke, he tried to ignore it. But the top-hatted Jewish greats could not ignore a joke that bordered on what was called *Majestätsbeleidigung* [*lèse-majesté*]. They must have tried to apologize for the behavior of one who was really not a member of the community but a sojourner from a faraway oriental country; this no doubt was followed by an official letter of humble apology.

The historical truth was as follows. The evening after the Kaiser's visit to the synagogue, Yahuda was invited to a dinner by Dr. von Renvers, a prominent Berlin physician. (He was physician to the Empress Victoria, mother of the Kaiser, to a Chancellor von Bülow and other members of the imperial entourage.) Naturally, the Kaiser's visit was the topic of conversation. After dinner the old General von Hugo (tutor of the Kaiser as Crown Prince) turned to Yahuda and said: "Well, this day must have filled the hearts of the Jews with pride, because the most high Lord (*allerhöchste Herr*) so graciously honored them by his visit." To which Yahuda replied:

"I view this incident from a historical viewpoint. Some 3500 years ago the Hebrews made bricks for a Pharaoh, now it is a Pharaoh that has made bricks for the Hebrews." A reference to the *Kadiner Kacheln*. Everybody laughed and the joke went from mouth to mouth. It would not be astonishing if the Kaiser, who was fond of Jewish jokes, was not informed of Yahuda's quip.

Another incident was reported by Yahuda: At the reception in the synagogue when the Kaiser was shown one of the Torah scrolls, he asked James Simon, financial advisor to the famous Deutsch-Orient-Gesellschaft, to read a few lines so he could get an idea of how the Hebrew text sounded. But neither James Simon nor any of the other Jewish dignitaries were able to comply with the royal request. The ruler was given to understand that the Scrolls contained the oldest version of the Five Books of Moses; they were written in the old Hebrew script and could only be read by rabbis and scholars. (However, no rabbi or scholar was invited to the reception.)[53]

Jews were expelled from Spain in 1492, but the exiles, especially members of noble families, never forgot their "origin." The Yahuda family well remembered their history. In the twelfth century it was their ancestor who represented the Jews at the court of Alfonso II. It must have been a special legislation that made it possible (in 1915) for Abraham Shalom to be offered a professorship at the University of Madrid. As a descendent of a distinguished Spaniard, he was ordered to present himself to the ruling sovereign, King Alfonso XIII. He appeared as directed but, in introducing himself followed his own, by then already highly developed, style: "I am not the first in my family who appears in audience before one of your majesty's family. It was in the mid-twelfth century, when one of my forefathers, Sheshet Benveniste,[54] had the high honor of appearing before your majesty's forefather, King Alfonso II." It is not known whether the King was amused or insulted by this intimate directness. Perhaps he marvelled at the historic sense of the visitor; perhaps he noted gratefully that the Jews had overcome the bitterness and the tragedy of the Expulsion. Yahuda's tenure at the University of Madrid ended in 1922.

In the following years he taught at a number of learned institutions, chiefly in England: King's College, University College, Universities of Oxford and Cambridge. He lectured at the Hebrew University in Jerusalem and at academies in Cairo and Lisbon.

His *Die Sprache des Pentateuch in ihren Beziehungen zum Aegyptischen*

(1929) in which he tried to prove a strong Egyptian influence on the language of the Pentateuch, was rejected by Spiegelberg and other Semitists — a source of much distress to Yahuda.

In the Nazi period Yahuda and his wife (an aristocratic woman from a South-African Jewish family) lived in London. Saturday afternoon was "open house" and many came to visit the famous scholar. The entrance hall was a rather darkish space. Prompted by Anne's father, I went to pay my respects. In the hall stood something formally elegant and stern and I stretched my hand out to greet the master. However, the something turned out to be a life-sized bust of Yahuda that, in the partial gloom of the atmosphere, looked like the real thing. Next time, of course, the bust no longer deceived me. What I did not fathom was the need for a life-sized dead bust if the living real thing stood in the reception room next door?

In 1942 Yahuda became a research professor at the New School of Social Research in New York. The means for their gracious living came, as before, from Yahuda's well-to-do wife. The year 1948 brought a deep disappointment in Yahuda's life. The Jews of the Land of Israel had been granted statehood, had bravely fought a war against their Arab neighbors, had chosen the name Israel for the new state (Ben Gurion's choice), and elected Chaim Weizmann president. Yahuda considered the choice of form of government to be a grave error. In most of the periods in history when the Jews enjoyed independence (or even semi-independence), the state was headed by kings, or priest-kings. Now, when independence was restored after so many centuries, Jews should have followed historical precedence and restored a kingdom rather than establishing a democracy headed by an elected president. And, Yahuda continued (in a conversation with me), there existed indeed a candidate for the throne of Israel: himself. Wasn't he descended from the Spanish-Jewish leader, Don Sosso Benveniste, who in turn preserved a sacred family tradition of its descendance from King David? In choosing a person of such august pedigree, the Jews would have re-established both their ancestral land and the legitimate Kingdom. Yahuda must have bemoaned the lack of trust in revered family records and the lack of will to follow hallowed traditions. He himself may have forgotten that a king of Israel was not elected by the people but chosen by God who made His will known by a prophet. Be this as it may, the Jews missed the chance to have a King Abraham Shalom the First.

The next (and last) stop was New Haven, Connecticut. There Yahuda hoped to find kindred souls, scholars to talk to, and to be admired by. He found (didn't he know this before?) that most scholars like to talk about their own work and about others only if they find something to criticize, or better, to tear down. Yahuda was lonely as never before. Knowing that some distant relatives lived in Boston made him take a trip there. He called us and we gave him a fine welcome; I tried to restore his faith in his scholarly accomplishments, especially in his contribution to a better understanding of the Pentateuch once the Egyptian linguistic element was realized. I praised the elegance of his Hebrew style – the relevant essays are collected in a separate volume. The friendly reception visibly delighted him. He imagined there must be more such homes in Boston where he (and his wife) would be equally welcome. He expressed the wish to move here, a wish that did not materialize – for whatever reason.

Yahuda died of a heart attack in Saratoga Springs, New York, where he was vacationing with his wife (August 1951). Mrs. Yahuda arranged with the funeral home in New Haven that the body be kept in a refrigerated vault. Daily she came and brought flowers to the deceased. After a few days a representative of the Jewish community appeared and implored her to allow her husband to be buried according to the Jewish rite. She refused, only to be approached again when a few days passed and Mrs. Yahuda persisted in her custom. Finally she gave in and a proper burial was arranged.

The following morning Mrs. Yahuda's body was found in her apartment. She had taken her life, to join her beloved husband in the beyond.

Harry Austryn Wolfson: Philosopher

When I first met him in the late thirties he was already uniquely famous among scholars. His knowledge of Jewish, Christian, and Muslim philosophies was incomparable and everpresent. Well known savants came to him for advice. His writings were of immaculate clarity, just as his pronunciation of English was a constant reminder of his Lithuanian origin. "Why do you talk with such an accent," he once said to the Brandeis philosopher Aaron Gurwitsch, "Why don't you talk like I do?"

In the thirties and possibly in the forties, Wolfson used to relax by going to a movie, preferably one showing a mystery or "who-done-it" (the two might be identical, for all I know). He used to invite Eisig Silberschlag (at the time a professor at the Hebrew Teachers College). The procedure (as

Silberschlag told me) was that Wolfson watched the first scenes, told Silberschlag who will turn out to be the villain or how the play will end, went to sleep right there, asking his companions to wake him toward the end, and watched the conclusion of the story to see if his prediction was right. Most of the time it was. Of course.

In his later years he was writing his *Church Fathers.*[55] That sounded like "Choych Fodders," or simply "di Fodders." The Divinity School did not mind in the least. The great seventeenth-century thinker was simply "Spinozzeh" and that was that. Sometimes a Yiddish word crept in. When Paul Tillich was appointed to the Harvard faculty, I chanced to meet Wolfson in the subway. "Have you heard about Tillich? Auch a Metzieh!" (What a bargain!). When on perfectly safe ground, he used Hebrew phrases which made sense only to one at home in rabbinic lore. Once at a Brandeis University banquet (where Anne and I had the pleasure of being his official hosts), he asked: "Where is here the 'somukh le-shulhoney' (i.e. that which is close to the table)?" He meant, where is the toilet? but the reference is to the Talmudic adage, "Who is rich? He who has the toilet close to his (dining) table" (B. Sabbath 25b). It so happened I knew not only the same reference, but also the location of the rest rooms.

In the mid-forties Wolfson had a nice little furnished apartment on Prescott Street in Cambridge. The place where he kept his choice manuscripts became legendary. It was the icebox, which for him had no other use. Friends advised him he needed a cleaning lady to keep the apartment in good shape; they even found a fitting person. The professor instructed her when to come and in which jar she would find the five dollars — the customary pay at the time. Wolfson deposited regularly the five dollar bill, trusting that the lady attended to her assigned duties. Weeks passed, and months. One fine day, the professor noticed that the bill resisted being pushed into the jar. An obstruction? No. Only that the jar was brim-full with five dollar bills and there was no room for a newcomer. The cleaning woman never came — the "occupant" was too strange a creature — and so the bills accumulated. Wolfson resisted any further advice how to manage his dwelling place.

Wolfson spent most of his time (if not all of his waking hours) in the Widener Library, Study K. Nobody who ever visited Wolfson will forget Study K. The rather large room was filled with books, journals, and manuscripts, some wrapped up in Yiddish newspapers. In the center were desks and tables; books everywhere. At one of the desks sat Wolfson – a little man, dwarfed by the vast expanse of books. Once he "boasted" that *Life* magazine, in an article on Harvard, gave his study more space than to the studies of his colleagues. He did not note that this distinction on the part of *Life* was due less to an appreciation of Wolfson's scholarship than to the amusing sight of the library. The whole thing made the impression of a disorganized, utterly untidy, disorderly assembly of material, a thing not expected from a Harvard savant. In reality, however, Wolfson was in complete control of his immense collection and could blindly pull out any little pamphlet he needed. This was something the *Life* editors could not possibly know.

Once he delivered a lecture at Brandeis University on an intricate point in medieval philosophy. He discussed the otherwise obscure meaning of a philosophical term in a given text and traced its history back to its origin and its use in later generations. Needless to say, he had no manuscript and no notes; the discourse flowed without interruption and the audience listened with rapt attention. After the lecture there was a dinner, at which a colleaque asked him how he ever arrived at his understanding of that obscure term. "I had a honch," he answered in all simplicity. Yes, in the case of Wolfson, even a hunch had the weight of a scientific proof.

In his *Philo* (1947), Wolfson demonstrated the importance of Philo's thoughts for the theological philosophy of the Christian antiquity and the Middle Ages. Erwin R. Goodenough, on the other hand, in his *By Light, Light: The Mystic Gospel of Hellenistic Judaism* (1935) and in other writings, treated Philo as a mystic and an interpreter of the Bible as a mystical document. Each one stuck to his presentation of the Alexandrian with vigor and a pronounced scholarly zeal.

Now the story goes that during Goodenough's visiting professorship at Brandeis University, he and Wolfson had lunch once a week together at Harvard's Faculty Club. They talked about every conceivable subject and every person within sight, regardless of whether they agreed or not. There was one subject both scrupulously avoided, though; for years it was close to the hearts of both: Philo. Each knowing the position of the other, it would have been not only impolite but outright dangerous to start a discussion. Harvard cultivates gentleness not only among the students but also in its celebrated faculty. In the case of Philo, no compromise was possible. To hell with *Veritas*. It is safer to turn to a genial topic, such as gossip about colleages or administrators.

As years progressed and Wolfson's eyesight declined, he could still find what he wanted but hardly read a desired passage. At one of my last visits to his Study K, he wanted to show me an alteration he made in the galleys (he pronounced it *galles*) of a book that was to appear in a revised edition. He produced the galley in question: "Read, read what it says here." I did, and sadly reflected that soon all this great scholarship and knowledge will have lost its author, its father.

Slowly the world of facts, figures, of the word, written or printed, of the correct version and correct view – all this moved away from him, isolated him more and more. But he clung to the world, however diminished, however reduced in size and range. He did not mention death but was fully aware of the approaching end. He used the phrase *seyvo ley teyvo*, a play on the words addressed to the patriarch Abraham that he will be buried in ripe old age (Genesis 15:15).*

The last days were spent in the Hebrew Rehabilitation House where the great man was given a private single room. The mind was clear, the memory strong, the will to communicate was as alive as before. Proudly he displayed a copy of the current *Atlantic Monthly*,[56] asking me to open to page so-and-so where his name was mentioned as one of the authors of this year's something or other. I admired the reference but silently wondered that it should matter to the great scholar to be mentioned especially now when he must have realized that the end was near. But, apparently, it was again that clinging to life – even in one of its most irrelevant forms.

The service took place in Stanetzki's funeral home. Rabbi Kazis and Professor Isadore Twersky, both students of Wolfson, spoke of Wolfson who lived in two worlds. The Jewish and scholarly communities showed respect, but only a few knew what his scholarship was about.

Jacques Lipchitz

His second wife, Yulla Halberstadt, was a friend of Anne's from Frankfurt. Later, after Yulla's marriage, the friendship was reestablished, and, naturally, extended to the master. I admired the great artist; he took to me as

*Hebrew, *be-sayvah tovah*

a person living in the Jewish tradition, so deeply important to him. I used to quote him midrashic phrases and passages that had relevance to his work. He liked specially the one of the statue which can be seen everywhere; a thousand men gaze at it, and it gazes back at all; so it was at Sinai: each one saw what his position allowed him (*Pesikta de Rav Kahana*).[57]* Lipchitz wanted to use it as an inscription for a statue he was commissioned to do for the Hebrew University at Mt Scopus.

He told that when invited to do a sculpture for a French church, he accepted under the condition that he inscribe the statue: "I, Jacob Lipchitz, a Jew, made the statue for the better understanding between faiths"– or something of this kind. The permission was given from Rome.

When he became gravely ill and the doctors were in doubt whether a cure was possible, Yulla (who had become thoroughly acculturated to the West and its ways) went to see the Lubavitcher rebbe in Brooklyn as a last recourse. Did she expect the rebbe to perform a miraculous cure? Just a prayer? Or, possibly, a personal reassurance by the saintly man? The rebbe received her at night: he let her describe the nature of the illness and what surgery was done or planned, and after a moment of reflection announced that Jacques would recover and regain his strength. And, the rebbe added, once he is on his feet again, tell him to come and see me. And so it was. The artist, advanced in years, recovered. When he appeared in the rebbe's residence, he apologized: "Rabbi, you know that I am engaged in work which is against the Jewish law." The rebbe advised him that there were many ways to serve God; his, Lipchitz's way was sculpture. Lipchitz must have thanked the rabbi for his help, and I presume the rebbe answered that it is not he who rendered help. In parting the rebbe requested that Lipchitz put on *tefillin* every weekday morning (and he gave him a pair of *tefillin*) and that Yulla kindle lights every Friday and Holiday evening. Not more.

Lipchitz became an adherent of the Lubavitch Hasidim and of course he and Yulla faithfully observed the acts required of them.

In 1969, in Los Angeles, Lipchitz's statue for the civic center was dedicated.**There was a reception and a public ceremony. The chairman engaged in a lengthy praise of the man who "made this celebration possible" and who, as his chief activity, manufactured a meat tenderizer. The speaker went into details of how beneficial the tenderizer was – and almost forgot Lipchitz.

*Chapter 12; edition of S. Buber, p. 110a. **Entitled, "Peace on Earth"

Suddenly, he reminded himself of the occasion, introduced Lipchitz and invited him to say a few words. There was time only for a very short speech. I guess Lipchitz did not mind. The local Lubavitch Hasidim used the opportunity of Lipchitz's presence in Los Angeles to organize a reception for him at the house of a well-to-do follower. Lipchitz felt at home and, attired with a skullcap, moved freely among the Hasidim and their hangers-on.

Years ago he and Yulla came to Boston as guests of Boston University, which gave a dinner in his honor. On the preceding evening we had the pleasure of having the Lipchitzes to dinner. Lipchitz was restless, for his suitcase had not arrived at the airport or could not be located. I attempted to set him at ease; we could let him have all he might need for the night, and the next day the luggage would surely arrive. That failed to answer his need; it turned out his *tefillin* were in the suitcase and he would need them early in the morning. I told him he could use my *tefillin* but he maintained he needed the ones the Lubavitch rebbe had given him. While we were talking the doorbell rang: the airline delivered the missing suitcase. At the end of the dinner Lipchitz applied to me the sentence from Scripture and from the Grace after Meals: "I have never seen a righteous man forsaken, and his seed begging for food" (Psalm 37:25). I did not want to reply that I have seen good men suffering and their children in need, and silently accepted his blessing.

When he died (in Capri, May 26, 1973), aged 82, but his work unfinished, Yulla contacted by phone the Lubavitch rebbe, who gave orders to his Hasidim in the neighboring city to take care of the body and accompany it to Jerusalem, where Lipchitz wanted to find his final rest. Yulla took comfort from the human concern and from the simple Jewish ritual as practiced by the Hasidim. When Yulla returned to New York she telephoned the rebbe to ask what should be done with her late husband's *tefillin*. The rabbi advised her to offer them to an Israeli soldier who may need them.

Yulla's sister in Zurich told me that Lipchitz much appreciated her and Yulla's father, the strictly observant Mr. Halberstadt. At one point he asked the old man to bless him.

Joseph Cheskiss of Brandeis

He was the person who negotiated the transfer of the grounds of Middlesex College to the group about to establish Brandeis University. He had belonged to the Middlesex Medical School that had fallen upon hard times and had become a Veterinary School; Cheskiss was the dean of humanities and was the last of the faculty to leave when the College finally collapsed. Or, rather, he did not leave but remained to represent the interests of the College that was ready to transfer the title to whoever was ready to assume it – free of charge. Cheskiss happened to know of the intention of a Jewish group to establish a Jewish-sponsored University – Einstein was a member of that group, or was represented by a secretary – and made the connection. The only condition for the transfer was that Cheskiss be taken over by the new group as a Professor of Romance Languages (that was his academic field). The location (in the neighborhood of Boston) was ideal, the grounds beautiful and sufficient for a small university. A point of special interest was the "Castle," a large structure built in the style of a fifteenth-century castle, erected by the original president of Middlesex College, a Dr. Smith, who wanted to impress the students with the grandeur of European civilization. The plan of the Jewish group was to tear down the Castle and use the ground for a more useful modern building. But the castle proved indestructible. And so it stands there, defying progress and utilitarianism.

To return to Cheskiss. He was a humorous, always curious person ("Nu, Glatzer, what is new?"), who made no attempt to hide his strong Yiddish accent. Yiddish was not only his background; it was his religion, his messianic hope. It is hard to imagine how he taught French with that pronunciation. In a discussion with a French scholar he interjected time after time: "Pourqva, pourqva?" with an appropriate gesticulation.

But I have to come to the point: In his living room hung a picture of an old Jew, possibly a rabbi. There is nothing to be said against this. However, around the picture i.e., around the shoulders of the old man a prayershawl was gently wrapped. When I first saw this I was astonished and – let me say it frankly – disgusted; later on I got used to Cheskiss's religious expression. Since he did not attend prayer services he, obviously, needed no *tallit*. But as a practical American, the *tallit* had to be of *some* use, had to have *some* function in the house. What better combination could be imagined than putting two and two together, or simply, let the rabbi use the *tallit*. The fact that the rabbi was not a live rabbi but a picture rabbi did not matter to a professor of literature used to symbolism. Or, maybe my interpretation is all wrong.

That Cheskiss followed his own logic and understanding of things was well illustrated when an official of the Committee for Refugees visited Brandeis and had lunch with the (then small) faculty. Suddenly, without any connection with what went before, Cheskiss announced his view of how to reform the salary structure of the faculty. "When a young instructor, or assistant professor, is hired, he should be given a full professor's salary. After all, he has a young wife, a few little kids — it is he who needs the money most. When the children grow up, he does not need so much money, so his salary is cut accordingly. Then, when the children are on their own and he and his wife start getting old, he should get an instructor's salary. What does he need the money for? For milk and crackers?"

The official was visibly taken aback. He saw it would have been futile to respond and changed the subject. A strange people, these Jews, aren't they?

When Alexander Altmann arrived at Brandeis, he happened to meet Cheskiss, who must have delivered one of his opinions. The next day Altmann asked me: "Is this man to be taken seriously?" Well, not in all things, but there were some things deeply serious to him: his belief in Yiddish, his negative view of the "nations of the world," his faith in the chosenness of the Jewish people. And perhaps, somehow and in the secret recesses of his heart, he may have believed in God.

When his son-in-law, Dr. Abelman, had to undergo a serious operation and the doctors doubted his survival, Cheskiss went around campus, asserting that "Got is a foter" (God is a father), which in this case proved true. Dr. Abelman recovered and Cheskiss took a walk around campus, triumphantly repeating, "Got is a foter, Got is a foter!"

Cheskiss's daughter, Josephine, fell ill and after a brief period of suffering, died. She was the mother of six children born to symbolize the six million that perished in the Holocaust. Difficult as it is to believe, to them, too, God was a father.

*David Daniel Glatzer,
father of Nahum Glatzer, c. 1925*

*Rosa Glatzer, mother of
Nahum Glatzer, Israel, 1951*

Matteh Aharon, Bodenbach, 1920

Glatzer with S.D. Goitein, 1923

Glatzer (standing, second from right), Breuer Yeshiva, 1925?

Nahum Glatzer and Anny Stiebel at the time of their engagement, 1932

Haifa, 1937

*Glatzer and son Daniel
Chicago, 1941*

Glatzer's 60th birthday, 1963, with Anne and Judith

With Jacques and Yulla Lipchitz, Italy, 1970

Glatzer lecturing, 1981

Brandeis University, 1968
Glatzer with
Abraham Sachar, Morris Abram,
and Yitzhak Rabin

January 28, 1972

124

III
Faith

How Are You, Tree?

Rosenzweig, with the help of his wife, told me this from his army service in the war:

Somehow they caught a Russian Jew wandering around and arrested him as a prisoner of war. He was put into a shed and watched day and night to prevent his escape. (Escape – whereto? Can a Jew find a refuge?)

He was brought to the attention of Rosenzweig; he, a fellow Jew, might interrogate him. Perhaps the man knew the enemy's movements, or planned movements, or anything worth knowing for the conduct of the war? (I am pretty sure he knew something of the wars of the Canaanites, the Amalekites, the Philistines, or even of the future wars of Gog and Magog – but who should have the slightest interest in the Russian war, as long as they leave the Lord's chosen alone?)

Rosenzweig noticed that the "prisoner" was quite sad and bewildered about why the goyim had to put him into that shed. In what he believed to be Yiddish (but in reality was but fractured German), Rosenzweig tried to console him: soon the admittedly strange war will come to an end and he will be free to return to mother Russia (oh God, what a mother!); in the meantime, why can't he enjoy the trees, branching out in all directions and providing homes for hundreds of birds? The trees, created on the third day, should be appreciated by man, created on the sixth day! "How nice," said the prisoner, "that a Jew knows *ḥumash* (the Pentateuch), at least the first 'Kapitel'; but *ken ich sogen, sholem aleichem, boym?* (How are you, tree?)"

Rosenzweig had no answer to this question, he told me. After all, this is indeed the gist, the most primitive expression of his, Rosenzweig's, philosophy of dialogue. Man was given language in order to use it and elicit response. God, too, speaks to man and thus "opens man's lips." Creation is voiceless, dumb. But man enters the scene as a speaking being. Mystics may talk to trees and rivers and mountains, but we simple humans must address ourselves to humans, or to a speaking and responding God.

I asked Rosenzweig whether at the time he noticed the similarities (regardless of its form) between his own "grammatical thinking" and the man's simplistic query. Yes, answered Rosenzweig.

(I do not know whether the story happened before or after Rosenzweig wrote *The Star*.)

Dayyan Posen

In Frankfurt nobody rivaled Dayyan (associate of the rabbinical court) Posen in piety and strictest observance. He is said to have been more pious than the Jewish rabbi in town, though that is hard to imagine. He succeeded in raising his sons to follow in his footsteps. One of them, in youthful folly, studied at a university and acquired the doctoral degree. When he matured he realized his mistake, shed his secular title, and forbade friends and acquaintances to refer to him as Doctor Posen.

But back to the father. It will do no harm to point to some less awesome traits in his life; indeed, it might help viewing the Dayyan's life in a more normal light.

His daily walk led him by the Liberal synagogue. He carefully avoided actually passing by the building; rather, he crossed the street and returned to the other side when past the synagogue. The scoffers in town knew the reason for this strange habit. They quoted the Dayyan saying: "Every day I pray this unholy building should collapse; but I don't wish it to happen the moment I pass it by." However, that sounds too malicious to be authentic.

Truer sounds the story of his scrupulous supervision of the bakeries to see whether the laws governing the banning of unleavened bread on the eight days of Passover were being observed. The Dayyan suspected a certain bakery was preparing bread on the last day of the Festival, to be ready for sale when the Festival was over. To find out, he scaled a wall that separated the bakery from the street. When he was almost finishing the ascent, someone grabbed him by the tails of his coat. It was a policeman. "What are you doing there, Rabbi?" asked the law enforcement officier. "Herr policeman, I am doing the same thing you are doing: seeing whether the law is observed!"

However, it is not always simple to establish a correct observance of the laws. A man came to the Dayyan to inquire whether a certain feed of a canary, advertised as "Kosher for Passover use," was indeed acceptable for a loyal observer of the laws. The Dayyan read the label, scrutinized the composition of the feed and the identity of the rabbis who guaranteed the ritual o.k. of the feed. Everything seemed correct from the strictly rabbinic point of view, yet a slight doubt prevailed and prevented the Dayyan from pronouncing an outright permission to offer the bird that particular nourishment. Finally came the verdict. "Please tell me, what does a Jew need a canary for?" I don't know whether the canary survived the verdict.

Addendum: In the early thirties, still in Frankfurt, a young member of the Posen family contacted me in considerable excitement: there was something of personal urgency which he wanted to discuss. He came and without much preliminaries declared that he planned to accept baptism. The Jewish Orthodox way of conduct and thought was no longer acceptable: there was more to life and to the world than the fulfillment of the commandments in all their exact detail. Christianity, he said, offered more of the freedom that is needed for an intelligent and mature pursuit of life.

I was not prepared for a discussion of an issue of such magnitude, but decided I must not fail the young man. The first step was to convince him that there is more to Judaism than Orthodoxy. There is the prophetic tradition, with its stress on justice and personal humaneness; there is the midrashic tradition of Hillel, Yoḥanan ben Zakkai and Akiba: humility, learning, martyrdom for the faith; there are the mystical ways of ascent of the soul to the region of the divine, and so on. As Jews we rose above the destruction of the Temples; we overcame expulsion and survived persecutions. We outlived humiliations, accusations of deicide, desecration of the host and poisoning of the wells. We learned to live in a hostile, harsh and at times brutal world and to preserve our humanity – and humanity in general – ready for a world of peace and mutual understanding. We called it Messianism; basically it meant having the courage to hope in a near hopeless situation. In the course of the centuries we lost not a few of our brothers and sisters who succumbed to the lure of a more secure realm in the Church. Those who arrived at the conviction that they need a mediator and that Jesus has come as the promised messiah and that the Church is in the sole possession of means of salvation – may they have found the peace they longed for. As for those who believe that the "Age of Faith" is a matter of the past, may they find a place in the secular world where they can practice their atheist or non-theist humanism.

Those, however, to whom Judaism still means something – however little – but to whom Orthodoxy offers too narrow a view, must respond to the question: Do I wish to be (or, to remain) a part of the Jewish people, accepting both the responsibility it places on its members and the freedom it offers? As members of the Jewish people we become brothers and sisters of Abraham and Moses, of Amos and Isaiah, of Jeremiah and Ezra, of Hillel and Akiba, of Maimonides and the author of the Zohar, of Deborah and Berurya, of the Baal Shem and the Gaon of Vilna. This contemporaneity of past masters, saints and sages, belongs to the mysteries of Jewish history. We do not allow persons and events of significance to become "historical artifacts." Memory is something sacred to us. In study and prayer, in festivals and fasts, our ancestors live.

Think it over, friend. Allow yourself time for reflection. Consider whether you really want to leave this community of life, of destiny, and yes, of promise. Promise: for we carry in us an ideal that will be realized in the world at large.

The young man sat there, silent. When he finally started to talk, it came out that he had spent years in traditional study of Talmud and commentaries, the Early Decisors and the Later Decisors, the super commentaries and glosses, but he saw no need to inquire what else is implied in the term "Israel." That was left to the reformers and Zionists. Now he realized, he confessed, that things are indeed different. He promised to do some further thinking. I was not sure whether I succeeded in shaking him a bit. I never saw him again. I hope he survived the Holocaust and could establish himself, in Zion or elsewhere.

Should I hope that old Dayyan Posen was spared the knowledge that at least in the case of one of his grandsons the rigid system of law and strict obedience to the divine statutes did not work and led this young man to near apostasy? Or should I be charitable and hope for the devout rabbi that he died in "old age and satiated of days," convinced that the following generations will not disappoint their ancestors and their faith. I prefer not to attempt to answer.

Reb Mendel

I once gave a lecture in the Zurich Jüdisches Lehrhaus on Franz Rosenzweig's view of history and especially, of Jewish history. The subject called for some abstract concepts (in counteracting Hegel and German Idealism) and the fanciful use of the term *meta-history*. I was not convinced that I did a creditable job but, on the other hand, I did not feel that I failed.

In the audience was Frau Margarete Susman, grand old lady and friend of Rosenzweig; she seemed to have been pleased with my talk.

Many years later (1971) I came to know Dr. Josef Guggenheim, a young, forceful community leader and son-in-law of our friends, Dr. and Mrs. Werner Wyler in Luzern. Guggenheim told me that Rosenzweig meant much in his intellectual life and that he read some of my writings on Rosenzweig. He mentioned that lecture and added that at the time he asked the rabbi of the community, Dr. Zwi Taubes, how he liked the lecture. Taubes was critical and explained to young Guggengheim why.

"When I was a child," Taubes said, "there was a pogrom in our little town; Jews went into hiding. When they emerged they found Reb Mendel with a big stick. 'Why do you need such a big stick?' people asked him. Reb Mendel explained: 'When the *meshiah* comes we will all go to Jersusalem. I am an old man. I'll need the stick to support me, for indeed I would like to reach that happy goal.'"

And Taubes added: "You see, that was strong, vibrant, living, hopeful, Judaism"— meaning that today, we have instead of that Judaism these abstract terms and lofty nebulous concepts ...

I thanked Guggenheim and told him Rosenzweig would have liked Reb Mendel and his Messianism.

The Rov

In 1944 Rabbi Joseph Soloveitchik (called "the Rov" by his followers and admirers) published in *Talpiot* a major article, "Ish ha-Halakhah" (The Halakhic Personality). The essay, written in a most beautiful Hebrew style, not only claimed for the observance of Jewish law the central place in Jewish life, but denied the — however circumscribed — validity of any other approach. The Halakhah demands a complete control of the Jew, to the exclusion of an emotional state of mind to accompany the halakhic function. There is no rightful place for, or justification of, a state of excitement or religious agitation, say, in the ceremony of blowing the shofar on New Year's Day; what matters, and matters exclusively, is the proper execution of the ritual.

This exclusion of the emotional side of religion bothered me when I read the essay. I planned a polemic reply but was dissuaded by my colleagues. I happened to visit New York and voiced my feelings to Professor Louis Ginzberg, the great Talmudist. I expected him to agree with me and object to the rigid stand of the Rov. The cautious Ginzberg did not wish to commit himself, or to say something that could be quoted as a criticism of his Talmudic colleague. He, therefore, did not go beyond saying: "I like my whiskey straight," which was a mild complaint against the Rov's combination of Halakhah and philosophy. The only reference that could be interpreted as an admission of esthetics into the realm of religion was Ginzberg's telling of the Gaon of Vilna (brother of Rabbi Abraham, Ginzberg's forebear in the seventh generation), who near death admired the beauty of the *etrog* that was brought to him, since the day was one of the Sukkot festival days.

(The Rov, apparently, would have felt: Never mind the *etrog*'s beauty. What matters is that the citron is without blemish and the benediction is properly pronounced.)

I was disappointed that Ginzberg did not wish to take seriously the younger man's question. In the meantime, the Rov changed his position and realized the wider dimension of faith. If you wait long enough ... Yet, even with the changed position on the part of the Rov, Ginzberg, were he alive, would insist on having his whiskey straight.

A Bit of Lubavitch Hasidism

End of the forties. I felt the time was right to introduce Daniel to Hasidism. No better place was there than the center of the Lubavitch Hasidim in Brooklyn, in walking distance from where we lived at the time.

It was the late afternoon before the onset of the seventh day of Passover. We arrived early. The congregation of the faithful was assembled; young and old readied themselves to commence the worship. We noticed that some Hasidim proceeded to the steps which, we assumed, led to the rabbi's apartment. We decided that that must be something very special and followed the select ones. One by one they were admitted to the rabbi's prayer room. I feared we would be expelled because of our non-hasidic dress and looks. But the doorkeeper must have realized that we were serious visitors and allowed us to enter.

The great rabbi was there and with him especially important followers. The noise of the multitude downstairs was audible; but the rabbi's sanctum was solemn, quiet; the prayers were conducted in a low voice. Two Hasidisms; one, of the simple folk, the other, of those who experience the glory of the Presence and are welcome guests in His Palace. Both are dependent on each other; each is in need of the other.

Thoughtlessly, Daniel touched the arm of the rabbi's chair. An angry Hasid rebuked him. One is supposed to show utmost respect and refrain from such vulgar intimacies. I wonder whether Daniel remembers this incident.

The following day we arrived at the rabbi's talk at the lunch table. The Hasidim listened with rapt attention. The kabbalistic exegesis of the scriptural portion of the day fascinated them. But not all of them. For suddenly one of the followers interrupted the mystical flow and shouted: "Rebbe, *mashke* (i.e., a drink)!" Apparently the booze was gone but more was needed to keep the spirit attuned to the rabbi's soaring heavenward. The attendants must have noticed the state of affairs, for in no time new bottles of whiskey appeared on the table. The rabbi was not diverted, nor disturbed. He may not have noticed what happened.

He should have. Daniel and I left the scene and took seats in the courtyard to observe the Hasidim coming in or going out. One of them, a heavy-set older Hasid in his traditional long black coat positioned himself near the wall and held his head. I thought he was in a kind of ecstasy. Nothing of the kind. He just vomited the schnapps before struggling on. My only hope was that my boy did not notice the disgrace, but he did and called my attention to the scene. My attempt to impress him with the piety of the Hasidim failed miserably.

The Little Gentile Boy

This is what Simon Halkin told me when we both lived and taught in Chicago. His mother was a strictly observant woman. She had engaged a little Gentile boy to come on the Sabbath to handle the oven (actually this, too, is not according to the law). The boy used to come, do his job, and receive a big piece of hallah, or white Sabbath bread, which he immediately ate with gusto. The pious mother used to say: "A rahmones auf den sheiketzel as er weist nit zu makhen a brokhe (What a pity that the little Gentile boy does not know to say the blessing)," i.e., he doesn't know the joy a Jew feels if before eating bread (or any food) he can turn in gratitude to his God.

She did not despise the boy for not being Jewish; she wished he could experience the bliss of Jewish observance, a bliss he so well deserved.

Bread is not just bread; if partaken of according to the custom of the fathers, bread becomes food from heaven.

131

Another attitude could have been one of pride (we have it, you don't), or one of envy (you Gentiles don't have to go through the ritual of pronouncing the correct benediction at every occasion; you are free). But in the case of Halkin's mother only one attitude was possible: compassion.

Prayer

From 1939 to 1943 I taught at the Hebrew Theological College in Chicago. When it became known how Jews in Europe – men, women, and children – were suffering, the heads of the College decided to have a special *minhah* service. Students and faculty assembled and recited the afternoon prayer. The minds and hearts of everyone were with our brothers and sisters, as if prayer could help them. But it did help to establish a communion out of which action could develop. In the course of the fervent reading of the prayers something changed in me. For the first time in my life I became aware of the reality of prayer – I do not find a better word. "One generation shall laud thy works to another and shall declare thy mighty acts ... They shall pour forth the fame of thy abundant goodness ... The Lord is gracious and merciful ... The Lord is good to all and his compassion is over all that he has made ... I shall speak of the glory of thy kingdom ... The Lord is faithful in all his words, and gracious in all his deeds ... The Lord is near to all who call upon him, to all who call upon him in truth ... The Lord preserves all who love him ..."

Suicide

The following was reported in the press some time ago. As I cannot forget the story I thought it best to write it down and perhaps then forget it. Do I really want to forget it?

A woman decided to take her life (no reason was reported), swallowed a large amount of sleeping pills, and went quietly to bed. Her husband had agreed to assist her. He sat down not far from his wife's bed and every few minutes rose to adjust her pillows, so as to make her position as comfortable as possible. There was no talk between them, no last words, no last good-bye; she allowed the poison to take gradual effect; he did his service silently, matter-of-factly. He must have realized that his wife was slipping away from him forever, but no attempt was made to rescue her in the last moment. But as long as he saw that there was life in her, he rose to adjust her pillows: the transition should take place as painlessly, as inobtrusively as humanly possible. To him this was not a cruel, ruthless, almost savage end of the life process, an end to love, to communication, but just a transition from one state to another.

The paper did not mention how long this process lasted. At one point the husband must have noticed that the end had indeed come, whereupon he must have notified the police.

I am unable to understand how a person can fail to approach life other than as a sequence of blessings and curses, achievements and failures, fulfillments and frustrations — all of them unevenly distributed. It is a person's duty to act in humility and hope that the last word will not be a fiasco but grace. Unless it comes in old age where a person is "satiated with days," death is always radically inhuman. To assist a self-inflicted act of dying is, to say the least, a highly questionable pursuit.

But we must assume that the man in our story wished to be charitable. We don't know what preceded the final scene and what followed. May he find forgiveness if indeed he erred.

The Child

This must have happened in the fifties, on one of my trips to Europe. I wanted to cross a street and waited for the green light, or for a lull in the traffic that would allow me to cross the street. Suddenly I felt a child's hand in my right hand. He (or she) too, wanted to cross the street and most naturally entrusted himself, or herself, to my guidance. Once we were on the other side of the street, our alliance ended, with or without a "thank you."

This little happening impressed me, for I took it as a symbol of a messianic future, as envisaged, for example, by Isaiah. The weak will be able to trust that the strong will not abuse his weakness, the strong man's hand will be open to receive in love his neighbor's hand, the mature will guide, the growing creature will follow, until he will be in a position to lead and to offer strength to others.

Where are you now, child? Did you retain some of your innocent trust or did you grow up to doubt, to suspect your fellow man, to distrust his motives?

Wherever you are, I thank you for the lesson you gave me. For I received many lessons in human evil, brutality, before you were born (was your father a Nazi?) and after. I have learned to protect myself against inhumanity (as much as one can learn this) and to avoid having to confront outbreaks of cruelty. But what you taught me was more important: to know that there exists trust, that simple confidence is a reality, and that it is worthwhile – yes, even imperative – to cultivate a heart open to kindness.

Reward

The doctor discharged me (January 1970) and I was free to go home. In accordance with a hospital ritual, I was not allowed to make my way on my own, but had to be helped down in a wheel chair, operated by an attendant. An older lady came to do the job. To show my appreciation I engaged her in a conversation. I asked her in what her work consists. She explained that she wheels patients to the x-ray room – some of whom are apprehensive; "so I talk to them until they are less tense. Some I bring in 'for treatment' and I see to it that they don't panic – which some do. Some very old people depend on me that I move them gently and avoid sudden turns which would make them dizzy. Each day presents new challenges and I try to do honest work." We arrived at the exit and waited for the car. I thanked her and said: "Your work is very rewarding." "Are you kidding? I make only __ dollars a week," and she mentioned her rather meager salary. That silenced me, for my reference was not to money but to an inner satisfaction of doing something to help those whose life was a burden.

To a person who grew up in Jewish ethical thinking, "reward" means an immaterial, and ultimately a heavenly, reward. No good deed should be done for the sake of material gain. The highest reward is "to sit (in Heaven) in the company of the just and rejoice in the divine presence." The helping old lady in the hospital was really a poor woman, for all she got for her labor was so and so many dollars, too few dollars. A poor creature indeed. My car came and I said a hurried goodbye. In my heart I prayed for the uplifting of her heart.

Two Faiths

Life magazine once published a full-page illustration of the Vatican's celebration of the Virgin Mary's bodily ascent to heaven. Utter solemnity of the ritual, stirring beauty of the sacred place filled with the faithful princes of the church in their vestments, lower clergy, dignitaries of all kinds, and perhaps some simple folk. The page in *Life* is mute, but one has the distinct sensation of hearing from far away the voices of the devout choir and the organ's awesome accompaniment. A miracle has happened: the mother of God is not allowed to rot in the ground, according to the law governing mortal man. Those present in St. Peter's may well imagine to see the Virgin ascend and rise higher and higher, with a gesture of blessing, until disappearing in the heavenly expanse.

The son of the Old and ever-New Covenant turns the page of the magazine. On the back page he is startled to see the illustration of a young Jewish couple in the corner of a waiting room of a railroad station. The woman sits at a bare table in the dimly-lit room; her sad, far-away look suggests that she is worried; the fact that she is highly pregnant indicates at least one of the reasons for her concern. Where will the little one be born? Will she have the milk to nurse the baby? How will the relatives – known by name and address only – receive them? Will the husband find work and be able to establish a home? She remembers her mother telling her in parting: Don't worry, God will help.

It can hardly be that *Life's* editor purposely contrasted the two pictures. What could be the purpose? To show the superiority of the adoration of supernatural event over that moment of realism in the daily life of a wandering people? Did he want to contrast two mothers, one elevated and one forsaken? Improbable in a magazine that has a distribution counting in millions.

Yet, here it was: two distinct faces of humanity. The pregnant women's husband stood there facing the corner of the room. Was this the direction to the East, to Jerusalem, as required for the Prayer of Benedictions? Never mind; the book says: *If you don't know the direction, direct your heart to our father in heaven.*

Blessed art thou, Lord, our God and God of our fathers ... He who acteth in mercy and bringeth salvation for His name's sake, in love.

O yes, there is divine kindness in the world; may we live to be granted a share in it.

Thou gracest man with understanding and teacheth the earthling wisdom ... let us return to thee ... and forgive us, father for we have sinned, thou, who multiplieth forgiveness.

135

I, too, have sinned against thy law, knowingly and unknowingly. I considered my advantage rather than thy purpose. In need, I looked around me for help and forgot thy presence. Let me return to thee.

Behold our poverty; give reward to all who trust in thy name, in faith; let our portion be with them.

Yes, our poverty. How will I find support for my wife and our baby? I don't desire much, just "bread to eat and a garment for cover," as our father Jacob said.

Return to Jerusalem, thy city, in mercy; build her soon in our days, o thou, builder of Jerusalem.

This is far off, but, I know, the day will come and we shall all be united in the holy city. Our baby — I hope it will be a boy — will study Torah there and become a sage and a teacher. We shall live there, secure and tranquil and none will make us afraid. So,

We thank thee for our lives which are in thy hand, for our souls committed to thee, for the miracles every morning and every evening; thy mercies are without end, thy love is without limit; from eternity we trust in thee.

Our wants are many and often we despair. But greater than want and despair is our gratitude for thy love and mercy. When I think of thee, I forget our destitution. The mentioning of thy name brings ever new hope.

Bring peace, goodness and blessing, love and mercy. Blessed art thou who blesses thy children with peace.[58]

The prayer must come to an end; the husband will take a seat next to his wife. They will talk of their immediate future: the chance to be accepted in kindness; finding some work; for her to give a safe birth to their child, and to have a home, dedicated to the service of God. Don't worry, God will help, as her mother had said.

Were the man whose mother was celebrated in St. Peter's to come to earth, and were he given the choice of joining the splendid assembly in the cathedral or the lonely, poor woman heavy with child and her husband, what would he have chosen? The old Jew in me tells me that he would have felt a stranger in Rome and much at home in the empty, cold waiting room.

136

Empty? No; there were human beings there. Cold? No; a warm loving heart spoke a prayer there.

The Black Church in Harlem

In the first year in this country (1938) I stayed at the International House in New York. One day a few of us decided to visit the Negro church of Father Grace. The service was in progress when we arrived. There was singing of hymns to the accompaniment of loud music that came from the left front corner. In the front center sat Father Grace on an elaborate chair. He did not move while the congregation grew more and more enthusiastic. Suddenly a man rose, made for the aisle, and in ecstasy moved to the rhythm of the music. Eyes closed, arms raised, the body contorted; he moved forward, to reach the presence of the cult's leader. Soon, more men and women rose from their seats and followed the first "dancer." The rhythm grew wilder and wilder, until over half of the assembly was on their feet. They all wanted to get close to Father Grace, and possibly to touch him, mystically unite with him. But this "aim" was prevented by the ushers who gently led the ecstatics away and back towards their seats. They each received their eyeglasses back which the ushers had removed from them when the matter became serious and there was danger they would hurt themselves. Back in their seats the jerky movements continued for a while until the ecstasy subsided and the worshipers became "normal." The participants had undergone a true mystical experience of the more primitive form. I was reminded of the prophetic gangs in the Bible that "inspired" the messengers of Saul and finally Saul himself. Nominally Father Grace and his followers are Christians; the Church wisely tolerates such deviations from the norm. Psychologically, I think, such dances which free a person from his or her sorry, troubled identity bring a much needed relief and offer strength, self-assurance and hope. We stood in a back corner of this church. After a while we thought we should leave, for the wild rhythm might catch us.

Kol Nidre at Harvard Hillel, 1978

The hall was full of worshipers, and so was the ante-room, the back hall and the gallery. The service was warm, devout, the students participated in the readings, responses and chants: a chorus of a thousand young, strong voices of men and women. When it was all over, the teeming masses filled the square adjoining the hall. Passersby threw a curious glance upon the strange assembly of greeters and well wishers. "These must be Jews, celebrating their Day of Atonement."

Some distance away, nobody was aware of the service, the worshipers, the holy day, the Jews. Even further away there was no indication that something would have warranted taking notice. The mass of Jews dissolved in the world around them; they became a part of the world again, just as they left the world behind when entering the house of God. They again took part in the world; as Jews they were suffused by a loneliness that was for an hour or two interrupted in prayer.

A Theological Dialogue

Fanya Scholem to me (in a discussion of political issues of the day): So — what will be?
I: We shall die — and live again.
Scholem: After three days.
I: Yes, Hosea 6:2. "We shall stand before Him."
Silence.

Father and Son

This was reported by a Nazi officer who was detailed to watch a group of Jews marked for destruction:

He saw a man talking to a young boy, apparently his son; the father pointed to heaven, as if explaining something. Soon they were gone but the officer could not forget the scene.

We know what the father "explained" to his son. He did not point to himself, in a gesture of pity, but beyond himself, there where the sky covered the whole earth, the good and the bad, the saints and the sinners. Know, my boy, there is something greater than ourselves; we are but tiny specks in the vast expanse of the universe; if we die, the light of the world will shine on; new children will be born who will continue where we left off. So do not be sad, my son, we are together. I'll accompany you to the last and praise God, "the true judge." If I should have to go first, I'll be happy to know that my seed survived me even for a short while. Over there, look, look, over there is the explanation.

The officer did not hear that; but we did hear it, and hear it over and over again.

138

Endnotes

Memories

1. Glatzer's formulation is not in accord with Slavic usage. For the present proposal we are indebted to Prof. Henry R. Cooper of Indiana University. A similar sounding Czech phrase, *obrad dvorsky* means "a court (or manorial) ritual, custom"; but this does not seem pertinent to the passage.

2. According to rabbinic legend, Miriam's well would "make its rounds" (*mitgalgelet*) or "accompany" Israel during its desert sojourn, providing the sustenance of water to the nation in recompense for Miriam's merits. See Midrash *Tanḥuma, Bemidbar*, 2.

3. "Tisha be-Av," *Jung Juda*, Prague, XXXI.13, July 9, 1920. See also "Father's Library" for the earlier submission (1918). Glatzer also published "Aus der Aggada zum 9. Ab," in *Weiner Morgenzeitung* IV, 1263, August 6, 1922.

4. Glatzer may allude to the teaching in *Seder Eliahu Rabba* 23, translated in his anthology *Hammer on the Rock* (New York: Schocken Books, 1948), 89 as "Meeting." It is taught there that "[T]he Holy one, blessed be he, finds man through love, through brotherhood, through respect . . . through a good heart, through decency, through No that is really No, through Yes that is really Yes."

5. Jacob Horovitz (1873–1939) studied at the University of Marburg and the Rabbinical Seminary of Berlin and later served as rabbi in Frankfurt. Although he was not a Zionist, he worked for the Jewish Agency beginning in 1929. In November 1938 he was imprisoned in Buchenwald. He died in Holland in 1939 of the aftereffects of his incarceration.

6. Frieda Kahn's memoirs were published as *Generation in Turmoil* (Great Neck, New York: Channel Press, 1960). She refers to Glatzer on pp. 116, 119, 144, 162f.

7. The phrase is from the liturgical poem *Yah, Ana Emtza'ekha* ("Lord, Where Shall I Find You"). It has been printed and translated in *The Penguin Book of Hebrew Verse*, ed. T. Carmi (New York: Penguin, 1981), 338f.

8. Recorded as a dream from the week of September 22, 1974.

9. Schocken Bucherei, 1935. Glatzer translated "Erzählung von Kopftuch," "Betergemein-schaft," and "Sabbath." The first of these also appeared in *Almanach des Schocken Verlags*, 5694 (Berlin, 1933).

10. ("The Outcast") Schocken Bucherei, no. 78, 1939. In 1937 Glatzer translated "Die Verlassenen" in *Jüdische Rundschau* 42, 6 and 7, January 22 and 26.

11. Husband of Glatzer's older sister Fanny.

12. Trade edition (Berlin: Schocken Verlag, 1933).

13. Josie Wechsler, Glatzer's granddaughter.

14. Brother of Anne Glatzer.

15. Wife of Franz Rosenzweig.

16. "Merksprüche aus Talmud und Midrasch," in *Jüdische Rundschau*, January–November, 1936 (25 sayings); January–September 1937 (14 sayings).

17. The work was published as *Hammer on the Rock. A Short Midrash Reader* (Schocken Books, 16; New York: Schocken Books, 1948), trans. Jacob Sloan. In the essay on Salman Schocken below, Glatzer refers to his unfulfilled desire to produce a more comprehensive anthology.

18. Published by Schocken Verlag, Berlin. The trade edition appeared the following year, entitled *Untersuchungen zur Geschichtslehre der Tannaiten* (Berlin: Schocken Verlag, 1933).

19. (Washington, D.C.: Hillel Little Books, 1956; 2nd edition 1957.) That same year Glatzer also wrote "Hillel the Elder in the Light of the Dead Sea Scrolls," in *The Scrolls and the New Testament*, ed. K. Stendahl (New York: Harper & Row, 1957).

20. Vol. 10.2 (1946).

21. Vol. 6.

22. Entitled *Der Friede: Idee und Verwirklichung*, ed. E. Fromm, et al. (Heidelberg: Lambert Schneider Verlag, 1961). The essay is reprinted in Glatzer's *Essays in Jewish Thought* (University, Alabama: University of Alabama Press, 1978).

23. See his *Essays in Jewish Thought*.

24. *Franz Rosenzweig. His Life and Thought* (New York: Farrar, Strauss, and Young and Schocken, 1953, 1961, and Hackett Pub. Co., 1998). Glatzer also published *Franz Rosenzweig: On Jewish Learning*, with Appendices by Martin Buber and Franz Rosenzweig (New York: Schocken Books, 1955) and many essays on Rosenzweig's life and thought.

25. *Leopold Zunz: Jude – Deutscher – Europäer: Ein jüdisches Gelehrtenschicksal des 19. Jahrhunderts in Briefen an Freude* (Schriftenreihe wissenschaftlicher Abhandlungen des Leo Baeck Instituts, no. 11; Tubingen: J.C.B. Mohr, 1964).

26. *The Letters of Martin Buber. A Life of Dialogue*, ed. Nahum N. Glatzer and Paul Mendes-Flohr (New York: Schocken Books, 1991). Glatzer also edited *The Way of Response: Martin Buber* (New York: Schocken Books, 1966), *On the Bible* (New York: Schocken Books, 1967), and *On Judaism* (New York: Schocken Books, 1968).

27. Glatzer edited *Parables and Paradoxes* (New York: Schocken Books, 1961), *Franz Kafka. The Complete Stories* (New York: Schocken Books, 1971), *I am a Memory Come Alive. Autobiographical Writings* (New York: Schocken Books, 1974), *Letters to Otla and the Family* (New York: Schocken Books, 1982), and *The Loves of Franz Kafka* (New York: Schocken Books, 1986).

Encounters

28. "Nathan Birnbaum über Wesen der Fromen im Judentum," *Israelit*, Frankfurt a.M., Nr. 13, March 27, 1924. Glatzer subsequently contributed "Sieben Gleichnisse und Legenden" to the Nathan Birnbaum Festschrift, *Vom Sinn des Judentums* (Frankfurt a. M., 1925).

29. According to a letter written to Buber on 6 Elul 5680 (August 20, 1920), Glatzer requested a meeting while in Berlin, where he stayed briefly with his mother's relatives en route to Frankfurt. The letter is in the possession of the family.

30. See *Martin Buber's Way to "I and Thou": The Development of Martin Buber's Thought and His "Religion as Presence Lectures,"* by Rivka Horowitz (Philadelphia: Jewish Publication Society, 1988).

31. See *The Letters of Martin Buber. A Life of Dialogue*, ed. Nahum N. Glatzer and Paul Mendes-Flohr (New York: Schocken Books, 1991), 306–10. The letter was unanswered directly, but referred to in a letter from Buber to Rosenzweig on November 14, 1923, and from Rosenzweig to Buber on November 20, 1923. For translations of these documents, see ibid., 310, n. 9.

32. See *Martin Buber. Briefwechsel aus sieben Jahrzehnten*. Band II: 1918–38, ed. G. Schaeder (Heidelberg: Lambert Schneider Verlag, 1973). The letter was written July 28, 1926. Glatzer's

translation here differs from that of Richard and Clara Winston and Harry Zohn in *The Letters of Martin Buber. A Life of Dialogue,* 344 ("The copy that young Glatzer has prepared is very clean and neat.")

33. (Philadelphia & New York: Jewish Publication Society & Meridian Books, 1958), 57.

34. Ibid., 54.

35. *Martin Buber. Briefwechsel,* 466f (The letter begins on p. 465).

36. Ibid., 479 (The letter begins on p. 478).

37. See *Die Schrift und ihre Verdeutschung* (Berlin: Schocken Verlag, 1936). The volume has been translated as *Scripture and Translation* by Laurence Rosenwald, with Everett Fox (Bloomington, Indiana: Indiana University Press, 1994); and see especially Rosenwald's essay on "Buber and Rosenzweig's Challenge to Translation Theory," xxix–liv.

38. For Glatzer's analysis of Buber's biblical work, see his "Buber as an Interpreter of the Bible," *Library of Living Philosophers,* Buber Volume, ed. P. Schilpp (LaSalle, Illinois, 1957).

39. *The Great Wall of China. Stories and Reflections,* trans. Willa and Edwin Muir (New York: Schocken Books, 1946; new edition 1970), with notes by Philip Rahv.

40. *Dearest Father. Stories and Other Writings,* trans. Ernst Kaiser and Eithre Wilkens (New York: Schocken Books, 1954), with notes by Max Brod.

41. *Description of a Struggle,* trans. Tania and James Stern (New York: Schocken Books, 1958).

42. Edited by A. Altmann (London: East and and West Library, 1958); reprinted in *Arguments and Doctrines,* ed. Arthur A. Cohen (New York: Harper & Row, 1970), and in Glatzer's *Essays in Jewish Thought.*

43. New York: Schocken Books, 1977.

44. See Hartmut Binder, *Motiv und Gestaltung bei Franz Kafka* (Bonn, 1966).

45. Odradek appears in "Cares of a Family Man" (1917). Kafka made up this Czech name for "a thread of spool that climbs up and down the stairs on two rods, a coiled phantom"; see Angelo Maria Ripellino, *Magic Prague,* trans. D. Marinelli (London: Picador, 1995) 33f. See idem, 34f, for a discussion of Kafka's interest in Czech language, literature, and culture.

46. See *Briefe an Felice und andere Korrespondenz aus der Verlobungzeit,* ed. Erich Heller and Jorgen Born, with an introduction by Erich Heller (Frankfurt a. M.: S. Fischer Lizenzausgabe, 1967).

47. In fact, the publisher's note (pp. v–vii) begins by referring to Baeck as "a representative figure of European Jewry," but also goes into a discussion of his wartime activities.

48. Glatzer's original account appeared in "Franz Rosenzweig: The Story of a Conversion," *Judaism: A Quarterly* 1.1 (1952) This was a prepublication of the Introduction to *Franz Rosezweig. His Life and Thought,* published in 1953.

49. Rome was married to Schocken's daughter Chava.

50. *Letters to Milena,* ed. Willy Haas, trans. Tania and James Stern (New York: Schocken Books, 1953.) The original appeared as *Briefe an Milena,* ed. and with afterword by Willy Haas (New York & Frankfurt a. M.: Schocken Books & S. Fischer Lizenzausgabe, 1952).

51. *The Passover Haggadah,* with English Translation, Introduction and Commentary based on the commentaries of E. D. Goldschmidt (New York: Schocken Books and Farrar, Straus and Young, 1953).

52. Entitled *Hammer on the Rock. A Short Midrash Reader,* ed. Nahum N. Glatzer and trans. Jacob Sloan (New York: Schocken Books, 1948). The verse from Jeremiah is cited with its Talmudic exposition (in B. *Sanhedrin* 34a) on the page preceding the collection.

53. In the *National Jewish Monthly*, December 1941, p. 119.

54. Sheshet ben Isaac ben Joseph, also called "Prefect de Pratis" (c. 1131–1209).

55. *The Philosophy of the Church Fathers* (3rd. rev. ed.; Cambridge, MA: Harvard University Press, 1970).

56. June, 1974, p. 98. The book is listed at the conclusion of the essay "Anatomy of a National Book Award," by Benjamin DeMott (pp. 94–98).

57. Glatzer selected this teaching for *Hammer on the Rock*. It appears there entitled "To Me the Word" (pp. 41f).

Faith

58. Glatzer has interwoven passages from the communal prayer known as the *Amidah* with personal devotions. This stylistic tour de force also gives insights into Glatzer's great understanding of the rhythm and depth of prayer. His translations further reveal these sensibilities.

Glossary

People

Agnon, Shmuel Yosef (1888–1970), the first Hebrew writer to win the Nobel Prize in Literature (1966). Born in Buczacz (Galicia), Agnon emigrated to Palestine in 1907 but returned to Europe in 1913 and spent several years in Germany, where he became a prominent member of the circle of East European Jews and Hebrew writers in Leipzig, Berlin, and Bad Homburg. After a fire destroyed his library and many of his own manuscripts in 1924, he moved permanently back to Palestine. Agnon's works often depict East European Jewish life, exploring the disintegration of tradition, generational conflicts, and Jewish identity in a changing world.

Altmann, Alexander (1906–1987), rabbi and scholar. Born in Kassa, Hungary, Altmann received his Ph.D. in 1931 from the University of Berlin. He served as a rabbi first in Berlin and later in Manchester, England, where he founded the Institute of Jewish Studies. In 1959 he emigrated to the United States, where he was appointed professor of Jewish philosophy at Brandeis University and director of the Lown Institute of Advanced Judaic Studies. Altmann's works focus on the history of Jewish philosophy and mysticism and include studies of Isaac Israeli, Saadya Gaon, and Moses Mendelssohn.

Arendt, Hannah (1906–1975), political and social philosopher. Arendt was born in Hanover, Germany and studied with the German philosophers Martin Heidegger and Karl Jaspers. She left Germany in 1933 and worked for the Zionist movement in Paris. Fleeing to the U.S. in 1941, she served in various Jewish cultural institutions, including Schocken Books, before being appointed professor at the University of Chicago and later at the New School for Social Research. Arendt is best known for her *Origins of Totalitarianism* (1951). Her report on the 1961 Eichmann trial aroused much controversy in the Jewish community.

Baeck, Leo (1873–1956), rabbi and religious thinker. Born in Posen, Baeck studied at rabbinical seminaries in Breslau and Berlin and later became the leader of Liberal Judaism in Germany. During the Nazi period, he served as president of the Reichsvertretung (the representative body of German Jews) until his deportation to Theresienstadt in 1943. After the war he moved to London, where he continued to serve as chairman of the World Union for Progressive Judaism. Beginning in 1948, he served intermittently as professor of the history of religion at the Hebrew Union College in Cincinnati.

Bergman, Shmuel Hugo (1883–1975), philosopher. In his student years as a member of the Bar Kochba circle in Prague, Bergman was greatly influenced both by Martin Buber and by the neo-Kantian school of philosophy. After his emigration to Palestine in 1920, he became the first director of the National and University Library in Jerusalem. Later he was appointed professor of philosophy at the Hebrew University, where he also served as its first rector.

Bialik, Hayyim Nahman (1873–1934). Poet, essayist, editor, translator, and cultural emissary. Born in an Ukrainian village, Bialik lost his father at the age of seven and subsequently received an Orthodox upbringing by his grandfather. He began to write Hebrew prose and poetry while attending the yeshivah of Volozhin, Lithuania; later he lived in Odessa, Warsaw, Berlin, and Tel Aviv. With the rise of Zionism and the revival of Hebrew, Bialik became the foremost poet of Jewish nationalism, forging a new Hebrew poetic idiom that was both literary and conversational.

Biram, Arthur (Yizhak) (1878–1967), Hebrew educator. An early member of the Zionist movement, Biram attended Berlin University and the Hochschule für Wissenschaft des Judentums in Berlin and taught classics in German schools before emigrating to Palestine in 1914. Settling in Haifa, he taught at the Reali, the premier high school in Israel, and was appointed its principal in 1920. Combining the highest standards of scholarship with an emphasis on discipline, order, and physical education, Biram received the Israel Prize for Education in 1954.

Birnbaum, Nathan (1864–1937), writer and philosopher. Born in Vienna of parents of East European origin, Birnbaum was a prominent intellectual whose life and thought were marked by several spiritual turns. In the 1880s, he embraced an ethnic definition of Jewry and coined the term "Zionism." Soon after the founding of the movement, however, he chose to focus instead on issues of Jewish cultural autonomy in the Diaspora. Later he found new meaning in Jewish religious practice. Gradually returning to traditional observance, he served as the first general secretary of the Orthodox Agudat Israel movement, refounded in 1919.

Breuer, Solomon (1850–1926), rabbi, author, and leader of German Orthodoxy ("Trennungs-orthodoxie"). After studying at the Pressburg yeshivah and at German universities, Breuer officiated as a rabbi in Papa, Hungary. The son-in-law of Samson Raphael Hirsch, whom he succeeded as rabbi of the Frankfurt Orthodox congregation in 1888, Breuer was a co-founder of the Agudat Israel movement and instrumental in barring members of mixed Reform-Orthodox communities from becoming leaders of the movement. In 1890, he founded his own yeshivah, which he directed for 36 years.

Buber, Martin (1878–1965), philosopher, theologian, and Zionist thinker. Buber's translations of hasidic tales into German and his monthly *Der Jude* (1916–1925) had a great impact on the Jewish renaissance movement in Central Europe. In the years following World War I Buber embraced a "Hebrew Humanism" and called, among other things, for Jewish-Arab understanding and peaceful coexistence in Palestine. Widely known for the concept of dialogue he formulated in *I and Thou* (*Ich und Du*, 1923), Buber became a leader of the Jewish spiritual resistance against Nazism. After serving as professor of religion at Frankfurt University for a short time, he emigrated to Palestine, where he became professor of social philosophy at the Hebrew University.

Buber, Solomon (1827–1906), successful businessman and banker and highly respected scholar. The grandfather of Martin Buber, Solomon Buber was born and lived in Lemberg, Galicia, where he spent much of his time and money publishing scholarly editions of existing Midrashim and reconstructing lost ones. His publications, including his introductions and annotations, constituted a veritable revolution in the production of reliable texts and continue to be utilized in modern scholarship.

Dinur (Dinaburg), Benzion (1884–1973), historian and educator. Dinur studied at Lithuanian yeshivot and at several European universities. He emigrated to Palestine in 1921, where he worked as a teacher and educator and later became professor of modern Jewish history at the Hebrew University. Dinur was one of the founders of the bibliographic quarterly *Kiryat Sefer* and the quarterly journal *Zion*. As a historian, he attempted to reassess the course of Jewish history from a Zionist point of view, emphasizing the continuous tension between Jewish Diaspora life and a yearning for redemption in Erez Israel.

Elbogen, Ismar (1874–1943), scholar and teacher. Elbogen studied at the Breslau Rabbinical Seminary and first taught Jewish history and biblical exegesis in Italy. In 1903, he joined the faculty of the Hochschule für die Wissenschaft des Judentums in Berlin and for many years was unofficially involved in directing that institution. After his emigration to the U.S. in 1938, he was appointed research professor simultaneously at the Jewish Theological Seminary, Hebrew Union College, the Jewish Institute of Religion, and Dropsie College. His major works include histories of Jewish Liturgy and German Jewry. Elbogen also participated in the creation of the German Liberal Jewish prayerbook.

Fromm, Erich (1900–1980), psychoanalyst and social philosopher. The son of a prominent Orthodox family in Frankfurt, Fromm participated in the study group of Rabbi Nobel and lectured at the Freies Jüdisches Lehrhaus of Frankfurt before he devoted his energies to the study and practice of psychoanalysis. In 1929, he became associated with the Institute for Social Research in Frankfurt and after his emigration to the U.S. taught at the International Institute for Social Research in New York City and at universities in the U.S. and in Mexico. In all of his work Fromm demonstrated his belief that religion is a response to deep-seated human needs, and that Judaism in particular focuses upon human rather than theological experience.

Ginzberg, Louis (1873–1953), scholar of Talmud, Midrash, and Aggadah. Born in Lithuania, Ginzberg studied at yeshivot in Kovno and Telz and at the universities of Berlin, Strasbourg, and Heidelberg. After his immigration to the U.S. in 1899, he served on the staff of the *Jewish Encyclopedia*. An important force behind the emerging Conservative movement in the U.S., Ginzburg joined the faculty of the Jewish Theological Seminary in 1903, and taught there until his death. As a scholar, Ginzburg focused on midrashic and talmudic texts. His *magnum opus, The Legends of the Jews* (7 vols., 1909–38) is a comprehensive analysis and presentation of Jewish legends relating to Scripture. The legends are derived from a variety of Jewish and non-Jewish texts and are compared to those of other cultures.

Goitein, Fritz (later *Shlomo Dov*) (1900–1985), orientalist. Descendant of a Hungarian family, Goitein studied at the University of Frankfurt before his emigration to Palestine. He taught from 1923 to 1927 at the Reali School in Haifa and from 1928 to 1957 at the Institute for Oriental Studies at the Hebrew University. In 1957 he was appointed professor of Arabic at the University of Pennsylvania. Goitein published documentary texts from the Cairo Genizah and is noted for his studies of the religious institutions of Islam and the cultural legacy of the Jews in Yemen. His *magnum opus* is the multi-volume *A Mediterranean Society*.

Goodenough, Erwin Ramsdell (1893–1965), historian. Born in New York, Goodenough began teaching history at Yale University in 1923, specializing in the study of Judaism in the Hellenistic period. His *Jewish Symbols in the Greco-Roman Period* (13 vols., 1953–68), a comprehensive collection of archaeological remains, opened the door to research on an area of Judaism previously known only in fragments and generally neglected.

Gutmann, Joshua (1890–1963), scholar of Jewish Hellenism. Guttman was born in Belorussia and first taught in Odessa and Vilna. He settled in Berlin in 1923 and in 1933 emigrated to Palestine, where he taught at the Reali High School in Haifa and later served as head of the Hebrew Teachers' Seminary in Jerusalem. In 1949 he became professor of Jewish-Hellenistic Studies at the Hebrew University. Gutmann was also a member of the editorial staffs of the the German *Encyclopedia Judaica* of the Weimar period and the Israeli *Encyclopedia Hebraica.*

Haas, Willy (1891–1973), essayist, critic, and translator. Born and raised in Prague, Haas moved to Berlin and edited the influential weekly *Die literarische Welt* from 1925 to 1933. With the rise of Nazism, Haas left for India, but returned to Germany in 1949 to join the editorial staff of *Die Welt* and become one of postwar Germany's leading critics and essayists.

Halkin, Simon (1898–1987), Hebrew poet, novelist, and educator. Halkin was born in Russia but emigrated to the U.S. at age 16. In 1932 he settled in Palestine and taught at a high school in Tel Aviv. In 1939 he was appointed professor of Hebrew literature at the Jewish Institute of Religion in New York and in 1949 professor of Modern Hebrew Literature at the Hebrew University. The author of *Trends in Modern Hebrew Literature* and a noted translator of works of English literature into Hebrew, Halkin dealt in his own works with themes of love, death, and the loss of religous faith.

Hertz, Joseph Herman (1872–1946), chief rabbi of the United Hebrew Congregrations of the British Commonwealth. A native of Slovakia, Hertz was the first graduate of the Jewish Theological Seminary of America. He served as rabbi in Syracuse, in New York City, and in South Africa before he was elected Chief Rabbi of England in 1915. The author of widely used commentaries on the Pentatuech (1929–36) and on the prayerbook (1942–45), Hertz was also a well-known public figure and one of the chief supporters of the Zionist cause in the debates preceding the Balfour Declaration (1917).

Hirsch, Samson Raphael (1808–1888), rabbi, writer, and foremost exponent of Orthodoxy in nineteenth-century Germany. Despite his friendship with Abraham Geiger, Hirsch opposed the assimilationist tendencies of the contemporary Reform movement, in particular its repudiation of Hebrew and abandonment of belief in a future return to Zion. He attempted to show (especially in his well known *Nineteen Letters*) that a modern secular education was compatible with adherence to the Law. But when he deemed the chasm between Reform and traditional Judaism irreconciliable, he opted for the separation of Orthodox congregations from the Jewish communities.

Horovitz, Joseph (1974–1931), orientalist. Brother of Jacob Horovitz, Joseph studied at the University of Berlin and taught there from 1902 to 1907. From 1907 to 1914 he taught Arabic and served as the curator of Islamic inscriptions for the Indian government. From 1914 until his death, he taught Semitic languages at the University of Frankfurt.

Kahn, Erich Itor (1905–1956), pianist and composer. Born in Rimbach, Germany, Kahn in his youth became a member of the Zionist Blau-Weiss movement. From 1928 to 1933, he served as director of the Frankfurt broadcasting station. He emigrated to France in 1933, and in 1941 to the U.S., where he was a founding member of the Albineri Trio.

Kaufmann, Yehezkel (1889–1963), essayist and biblical scholar. Kaufmann studied at modern yeshivot in Russia and after World War I moved to Berlin. In 1928 he emigrated to Palestine, where he taught at the Reali High School in Haifa until his appointment as professor of Bible at the Hebrew University in 1949. Kaufmann's major scholarly works deal with the problem of exile in Jewish history.

Landauer, Gustav (1870–1919), philosopher and writer. Born in Karlsruhe, Landauer wrote for the anarchic-socialist periodical *Sozialist* throughout his life. A free lance journalist, he was imprisoned several times for incitement. With Martin Buber, he formed an international organization dedicated to averting world war through individual responsibility. Influenced by Buber, he gradually developed a more positive attitude to Jews and Judaism. A leader of the Bavarian Soviet Republic, he was brutally murdered by counterrevolutionary soldiers.

Lewisohn, Ludwig (1882–1955), novelist and critic. Born in Berlin, Lewisohn came to the U.S. in 1890, studied at Columbia University, and became professor of German at Ohio State. A pacifist with pro-German sympathies, he was forced to abandon his teaching position during World War I and returned to academia only after World War II, when he became deeply interested in Zionism. In 1948, Lewisohn was appointed professor of comparative literature at Brandeis, where he was a colleague of Glatzer. Among his best known works is *The American Jew: Character and Destiny*.

Lipchitz, Jacques (Chaim Jakob) (1891–1973), sculptor. Born in Lithuania, Lipchitz went to Paris in 1909 and became one of the foremost cubist sculptors. During the mid 1920s his work developed into a more figurative, emotional, and metaphoric style, and he frequently derived inspiration from biblical motifs. In 1940, he fled to southern France and then to New York. On his eightieth birthday, he donated a large set of bronzes from his Paris work to the Israel Museum in Jerusalem.

Loewe, Herbert (1882–1940), English orientalist. Loewe completed his studies at Cambridge and then held teaching positions in the Middle East. After his military service in India, he taught rabbinics at Oxford, Cambridge, and the University of London. Representing informed and tolerant Orthodoxy, Loewe was a leader of British scholarly Jewry, and his home was a center of Jewish life.

Magnes, Judah Leon (1877–1948), rabbi, communal leader, and university president. Born in California and ordained a Reform rabbi in 1900, Magnes became a major communal leader in the U.S. and an early supporter of Zionism. His U.S. career faltered in 1917 because of his outspoken opposition to the U.S. entry into World War I. He emigrated to Palestine in 1922, participated in the establishment of the Hebrew University, and became its first chancellor (1925–35) and first president (1935–1948). His pacifist convictions led to a life-long commitment to Arab-Jewish understanding.

Nobel, Nehemia Anton (1871–1922), Orthodox rabbi and religious leader. Of Hungarian descent, Nobel was educated in Germany and studied at the Orthodox Rabbinical Seminary of Berlin. He served in the rabbinates of Cologne, Leipzig, Hamburg, and Frankfurt, and in 1919 became president of the General Rabbinical Association of Germany. In contrast to the anti-Zionism then prevalent among German rabbis, Nobel was devoted to the Zionist cause and a close friend of Theodor Herzl. In the last decade of his life, Nobel figured as a charismatic personality among the Jewish intellectuals of Frankfurt, often drawing several hundred students to his lectures at the Freies Jüdisches Lehrhaus.

Persitz, Shoshana (1893–1969), publisher and politician. Born in Kiev, Persitz became a leading figure in the Tarbut Hebrew language movement in Russia. After moving to Germany in 1920, she played an active role in the brief flourishing of Hebrew culture in Weimar Germany. Together with her husband, Persitz established the Omanut publishing house in Moscow, in Frankfurt, and later in Palestine. After the establishment of the State, she served as a member of the Knesset and was awarded the Israel Prize in education in 1968.

Plessner, Martin (Meir) (1900–1973), orientalist and Islamic scholar. Plessner became professor at the University of Frankfurt in 1931. In 1933 he emigrated to Palestine and was appointed professor of Arabic language and literature at the Hebrew University in 1955. His fields of specialization were the history of Islamic science and the influence of Islamic classical heritage on medieval Judaism.

Rosenzweig, Franz (1886–1929), theologian and philosopher. Born into an acculturated German Jewish family, Rosenzweig was on the brink of converting to Christianity when he "rediscovered" Judaism in 1913 during an Orthodox High Holiday service in Berlin. He began writing his major work *The Star of Redemption* while serving as a German soldier in World War I. The book develops a "New thinking" in philosophical theology, based on the triad of creation, revelation and redemption. After the war, Rosenzweig devoted most of his energies to the renewal of Jewish education, realizing an idea he called the New Learning. In contrast to the Old Learning, which started from the Torah and led into life, the New Learning had to lead from the world of alieniated Jews back to the Torah. From 1921 Rosenzweig suffered from a progressive paralysis that ultimately immobilized him completely. In spite of his condition, he produced in his last years many translations of Hebrew works into German, including a Bible translation with Martin Buber.

Schocken, Salman (1877–1959), Zionist and publisher. Schocken founded and developed a prosperous chain of department stores before he became a major publisher of general and Hebrew literature. He was a patron of S.Y. Agnon and the publisher of his works. In 1929 he founded the Research Institute for Hebrew Poetry in Berlin, which was transferred to Jerusalem in 1934. The German Schocken Verlag, established in 1931, was distinguished for its innovative Judaica series. Schocken emigrated to Palestine in 1934 and to the United States in 1940 and established publishing houses in both countries. He was chiefly responsible for the publication of Franz Kafka's works in America.

Scholem, Gershom Gerhard (1897–1982), pioneer and leading scholar in the field of Jewish mysticism. Born into an assimilated German-Jewish family in Berlin, Scholem joined the Zionist movement as a young student and henceforth devoted himself to a full understanding of the historical, religious, and cultural tradition of Judaism. His doctoral thesis on the book *Bahir*, completed in 1922, was one of the first serious scholarly works on the long-neglected and misinterpreted mystical tradition of the Kabbalah. Scholem emigrated to Palestine in 1923 and served first as librarian and lecturer at the Hebrew University and ultimately as professor of Jewish Mysticism and Kabbalah. A bibliography of his writings lists over five hundred items, including his classic *Major Trends in Jewish Mysticism.*

Simon, Akiba Ernst (1899–1988), educator, religious thinker, and writer. Born in Berlin, Simon was an active Zionist and close associate of Martin Buber with whom he co-edited *Der Jude.* He also taught at the Frankfurter Jüdisches Lehrhaus. After his emigration to Palestine in 1928, he worked as a teacher and co-director of secondary schools and seminaries. At Buber's urging, Simon returned in 1934 to Nazi Germany to help organize Jewish adult education programs. In 1935 he joined the faculty of Hebrew University, where he became a professor of philosophy and history of education. A religious humanist, Simon was an active member of virtually every group advocating a bi-national state in Palestine and equal economic rights for Arabs.

Soloveitchik, Joseph Dov (1903–1993), U.S. Orthodox rabbi and religious philosopher. The descendant of a well known Lithuanian rabbinical family, Soloveitchik received a thorough education in Talmud and halakhah before he earned a doctorate in philosophy at the University of Berlin. In 1932 he emigrated to the United States, where he became a leader of the Orthodox Jewish community of Boston. In 1941 he was appointed professor of Talmud (and later also of Jewish philosophy) at Yeshiva University. The unchallenged spiritual leader of enlightened North American Orthodoxy, Soloveitchik was popularly known as "The Rav." In his best known work, *Ish ha-Halakhah*, he maintains that only through the observance of the halakhah can a Jew attain true "nearness to God."

Susman, Margarete (1874–1966), German essayist and poet. Born in Hamburg, Susman later lived in Frankfurt, and from the Nazi period on, in Zurich. Combining scholarship and existentialist philosophy, she published several verse collections and essays on biblical figures. Among her best-known works is *Das Buch Hiob und das Schicksal des jüdischen Volkes* ("The Book of Job and the Fate of the Jewish People," 1946).

Tillich, Paul (1886–1965), preeminent Protestant philosopher and theologian. A vehement opponent of Nazism, Tillich was dismissed from his university position in Germany in 1933. Emigrating to the U.S., he subsequently taught at the Union Theological Seminary, Harvard University, and the University of Chicago. Tillich maintained close friendships with Jewish refugees from his native Germany and was one the first Christian theologians to promote dialogue between Christians and Jews. Among his major works is *Systematic Theology* (1951–63).

Weltsch, Robert (1891–1982). Zionist editor and journalist. As a student, Weltsch joined the Zionist students' Bar Kochba society in Prague. From 1920 to 1938 he served as editor of *Die Jüdische Rundschau*, the organ of the Zionist Federation of Germany. He settled in Jerusalem in 1938, where he edited a German language weekly. His 1933 article "Tragt ihn mit Stolz, den gelben Fleck" ("Wear It with Pride, The Yellow Badge") inspired many German Jews to return to Jewish values.

Wolfson, Harry Austryn (1887–1974), historian of philosophy. Born in Belorussia, Wolfson emigrated to the U.S. at the age of 16. In 1915 he received his doctorate from Harvard and was appointed to the Harvard faculty. In 1925 he became professor of Hebrew literature and philosophy. Wolfson mastered and wrote about philosophic literature in several languages, using a method of textual study he called "hypothetico-deductive." His major works include books on Philo and Spinoza, whose philosophical systems he held to mark the beginning and the end of medieval philosophy.

Yellin, David (1864–1941), teacher, writer, scholar, and leader of the *yishuv* in Palestine. Born in Jerusalem to a family of mixed Ashkenazi and Sephardi origins, Yellin participated in the establishment of the Hebrew Teachers' Seminary in Jerusalem and the National Library. He was a member of the Hebrew Language Committee, attended Zionist Congresses, and wrote textbooks and studies that promoted the development and teaching of modern Hebrew. In 1926 Yellin was appointed professor of Hebrew poetry of the Spanish period at the Hebrew University.

Zunz, Leopold (1794–1886), German-Jewish scholar and one of the founders of the Science of Judaism (Wissenschaft des Judentums), which sought to reexamine the Jewish cultural and religious heritage, subject it to modern research methods, and put it into historical perspective. Zunz's works laid the groundwork for the recognition of Jewish history as an inseparable part of the history of human culture in general. After his death his literary estate became part of the *Hochschule* for the Science of Judaism in Berlin. In 1939 the archives were moved to Jerusalem and became part of the National and University Library.

Institutions/Organizations

Agudat Israel (Hebrew: "Association of Israel"), world Jewish movement and later political party. Agudat Israel was established in 1912 to preserve Jewish Orthodoxy and protect it from contemporary trends towards assimilation, secularism, Zionism, and religious reform. Its initial membership drew from German neo-Orthodoxy, Hungarian Orthodoxy, and the Orthodox Jews of Poland and Lithuania.

Bar-Kochba Society, an organization of Jewish university students in Prague. Founded in 1893, its meetings subsequently served as forums for Zionist intellectual activities, particularly in the years preceding World War I. Martin Buber delivered his *Three Addresses on Judaism* before this group in 1909 to 1911, influencing it greatly.

Blau-Weiss ("Blue-White"), the first Jewish youth movement in Germany. Founded in 1912, it was influenced by the German Wandervogel youth movement, whose emphasis on nature, folk traditions, and collective experience it shared. During the early 1920s, the organization engaged increasingly in Zionist activities and many of its members, most of whom were from assimilated families, emigrated to Palestine. The movement dissolved in Germany in 1929.

Brandeis University, Waltham, Massachusetts, the first nonsectarian Jewish-sponsored university in the U.S. Founded in 1948, it was named for the U.S. jurist Louis Dembitz Brandeis, the first Jew to be appointed to the U.S. Supreme Court. The university is particularly known for its Near Eastern and Judaic Studies Department, which Nahum Glatzer chaired from 1953 to 1970.

Bücherei des Schocken Verlags, title of a Judaica series published in Berlin by the Schocken Verlag between 1933 and 1938. The slim volumes in the series were carefully selected to represent the essence of Jewish knowledge without demanding that readers be familiar with the Jewish tradition. The series became a vehicle for the dissemination of knowledge about Judaism for German Jews after the rise of Nazism.

Freies Jüdisches Lehrhaus. Founded in 1920 in Frankfurt by Franz Rosenzweig, the Lehrhaus attempted to revive Jewish learning among a largely assimilated German Jewry. It offered lecture series and study groups on various aspects of Jewish history and liturgy, the Hebrew language, and classical Jewish texts. After 1926, the Lehrhaus suspended its public function except for a few study groups. It re-opened in 1933, however, and, under the guidance of Martin Buber, became a center of Jewish spritual resistance to Nazism.

Hebrew University of Jerusalem. The university was founded on Mount Scopus in 1925 with two primary goals: to reconstruct the Hebrew tradition in its original language in the context of general humanities, and to provide a center for research in the natural sciences, which in turn would foster the development of the land. The campus moved to Giv'at Ram after 1948, when Mount Scopus became a demilitarized Israeli area within Jordanian territory. Since 1967, both campuses have been used.

Hochschule für die Wissenschaft des Judentums. After attempts to establish a professorship for Jewish Studies at a German university failed, the Hochschule was established in Berlin in 1872 to provide a site for the scientific study of Judaism. In subsequent years it became a seminary for training rabbis and religious school teachers, mostly of Liberal orientation. During the Nazi period, the Hochschule became a center for Jewish spiritual resistance. Forcibly closed in July, 1942, it was one of the few remaining Jewish educational institutions in Germany.

Jüdische Rundschau, journal of the Zionist Federation in Germany (*Zionistische Vereinigung für Deutschland*). Established in 1896 and edited by Robert Weltsch since 1919, the journal appeared twice weekly and continued publication into the the Nazi period, until it was forced to cease publication in 1938.

Jung Juda. The term *jungjüdische Bewegung* (Young Jewish Movement) was probably coined by Martin Buber around 1900 and referred to a small circle of Jewish artists and cultural Zionists who stressed the preeminent role of art in the creation of a modern Jewish culture and national consciousness. The movement was influenced by Nietzschean thought and by the cultivation of youthfulness and vitality characteristic of fin-de-siècle Central Europe. Jewish student circles identifying with the movement called themselves *Jung Juda*.

Other Annotations

Mendelssohn Bible, the Hebrew Bible translated into German by Moses Mendelssohn. It was printed in Hebrew characters together with the original Hebrew and a Hebrew commentary (called the *Biur*). Among the books Mendelssohn translated himself are the Pentateuch (1783) and the Psalms (1785–91). The project was later completed by other scholars.

Montefiore and Loewe's Rabbinic Anthology, A Rabbinic Anthology, ed. Herbert Loewe and Claude Montefiore. Published in 1938, the work presents rabbinic teachings with extensive notes by its two editors, the Liberal Montefiore and the Orthodox Loewe.

Makleff Family, pioneers in Palestine. Originally from the Grodno district of Russian Poland, Aryeh Leib Makleff emigrated in 1891 and eventually settled in Moza, where he worked as an agricultural expert. Despite his cordial relations with the sheik of the nearby Arab village, Moza was attacked in the 1929 riots and the family all killed except for the youngest son, Mordecai, who grew up to become Chief of Staff of the Israel Defense Forces.

Places

Buczacz: southwest of Lemberg

Lemberg: in 1919 part of the Austrian-Hungarian empire (Galicia); from 1919 to 1944 Poland; today Lvov, Ukraine

Glatz: town in Silesia, south of Breslau; in 1945 part of Germany (Prussia); today Klodzko

Ungarisch Brod: town in southeastern Czech lands; today Uhersky Brod; in 1919 part of the Austrian-Hungarian empire; from 1939 to 1945, Germany

Tetschen: in 1918 part of the Austrian-Hungarian empire (Bohemia); from 1939 to 1945, Germany; today Děčín, Czech Republic

Bodenbach: a few miles west of Tetschen; in 1918 part of the Austrian-Hungarian empire (Bohemia); from 1939 to 1945 Germany; today Podmokly, Czech Republic

Elberfeld: in Germany, at the Wupper river, east of Düsseldorf

Heppenheim: in Germany, south of Frankfurt